The Florida Symphony Orchestra

A Silver Anniversary History

by
Ruth Gilbert Smith

The Florida Symphony
Society, Inc.

P.O. Box 782
Orlando, Florida 32802

Printed in the United States of America

Cover Art: Jeffrey P. Paison
Printing: Cowart's Rollins Press
           Winter Park, Florida 32789
Graphics: Karen Heebner

PREFACE

*"Music once admitted to the soul becomes a sort of spirit,
and never dies; it wanders perturbedly through
the halls and galleries of the memory, and is often
heard again distinct and living as when
it first displaced the wavelets of the air."*

— Bulwer-Lytton

The Florida Symphony Orchestra is celebrating its Silver Anniversary, and what a shining event this is! During the past twenty-five years the Symphony has come from there to here, and in its progress has had many peaks and valleys. But it has arrived triumphantly, soundly community supported, and with its reputation extending far beyond this area. There is, indeed, much to celebrate.

There are facts and stirring events to be remembered, there are the intangibles — frustrations, disappointments, hopes, glories, exaltations. How does one describe an emotion? How does one write a history of a musical experience with so many variables?

Confronted by huge, stacked-to-the-ceiling scrapbooks filled with newspaper clippings, letters, programs and pictures relating accomplishments, ideas that clicked, some that died a-borning — where does one start?

To bring coherent order out of all this memorabilia digging the essence from all the diverse and ambitious planning, the hard work, the organization, the recruitment of workers, the raising of the ever-mounting annual budgets to provide the ever-growing quality and excellence of the Symphony to satisfy the demands and the needs of the fabulously enlarged community, will be an audacious yet awesome task.

It's like trying to grasp a mountain of dreams, with one gossamer peak slipping through your fingers as a brighter one beckons. You feel you are using a thaumotrope — that optical toy in which pictures on opposite sides of a card appear to blend together when the card is rapidly twirled. Magic!

And there's the typewriter, waiting to convince a busy practical world full of busy practical people that hundreds of them actually participated in this magical happening!

As you start with much pride to mark the years from 1950 to 1975 as the Florida Symphony Orchestra rose from its modest beginning to its present eminence, you have a faint memory of even earlier times, and think that perhaps you might well be calling this the fiftieth anniversary rather than the twenty-fifth. But we'll come to that later.

This will be a chronicle in which many people can accept their share of praise. In addition to those who were in official positions in the orchestra's organization, there have been hundreds — probably thousands — of men, women and children who have worked hard to insure the orchestra's success. These music lovers live not only in the Orlando-Winter Park area but in many other towns and cities where the orchestra has performed to enthusiastic audiences.

There is no record of the endless hours spent in planning, fund-raising, publicity activities, neglect of personal responsibilities in order that the Symphony might realize its potential.

The Florida Symphony Orchestra owes much of its well-earned fame, of course, to the brilliant musical conductors who, with skill and innovative knowledge, have directed their fine, well-chosen professional musicians to such heights.

The audiences who have attended the many concerts have contributed their enjoyment and appreciation, and their word-of-mouth advertising which helped spread the good news to others who had not yet heard the Symphony.

The idea of a Symphony Orchestra had to be sold to the business and financial community, whose idea of attracting desirable new industries and residents ran more to sports stadiums and recreational facilities than to concert halls and art galleries. Some "thought well" of symphonic music, but doubted that hard-headed captains of industry would consider it as anything more than an esoteric extra which might please a few specially trained individuals. They now admit that it came as a surprise when they were often questioned by prospective employees as to what this area had to offer their families in the way of opportunities for continuing cultural education and enjoyment.

The Florida Symphony, not only as a result of its ever-growing numbers of concerts, but also as a result of the wide range of symphony-related activities, has become the cultural cornerstone of Central Florida. Its impact is so great, and its services so broad, that it is difficult, now, even to imagine what life would be without the orchestra.

> *Music hath charms to soothe*
> *the savage breast,*
> *To soften rocks, or bend a knotted oak.*

> — *William Congreve*

What is a symphony orchestra, anyway? It has been called one of the most specialized group activities in existence, which is a good description. Individual musicians, with diverse musical backgrounds and ideas, must think as one — respond as one — and share the same discipline, if superb music is to be the result. There is romance, and humor, and hard work, before there is acclaim.

The Florida Symphony Orchestra has had its share of all those things. And though great care has been taken to research and prepare this story of the first twenty-five years of a great symphony orchestra, there will still be regrettable omissions. There may also be inaccuracies because of errors in source material. If errors there be, the information may be reported to the Business Manager of the Florida Symphony Orchestra, Inc., P.O. Box 782, Orlando, Florida, 32802, for use in future revisions of this book. Please make any report in writing, and sign the source, for assuring its authenticity.

It is a pleasure to share with you the Symphony story of the past quarter century [or half-century, as the case may be], during which you and I probably worked together, happily, on a project in which we both believed. Because this isn't just a story about a musical organization — it is also a story about love.

Ruth Gilbert Smith
January, 1975

THE SETTING — WHERE IT ALL HAPPENED

"Music is the universal language of mankind."
— Longfellow

Orlando is known for many things. None gainsay its beauty and its advantages - with its many landscaped lakes; its beautiful homes; its impressive City Hall; its tall new office buildings, banks, condominiums, apartment houses; its many excellent shopping centers with big, nationally-known department stores and boutiques carrying the finest of merchandise; its network of highways, making it a city accessible from any part of the state. The largest city in the area, located in almost the exact geographical center of the state, Orlando has much to offer. No wonder it has attracted nationally-known industries, and is surrounded by tourist attractions - Disney World, Sea World, Circus World, horse-racing tracks, trotting-race tracks, greyhound racing, a Jai Alai Fronton, and more.

Orlando has an excellent school system, an exceptional library system which rates with the best in the Southeast, beautiful churches of almost every denomination, a busy social life with golf and swimming and tennis as well as parties and dancing at the many Country Clubs, social clubs, civic clubs, and long-time associations of friends with their special interests - reading and book-reviewing, card playing, dancing, dinner theaters, travel, community interests, politics, antique collecting, and a myriad of other absorbing activities.

Orlando is a cosmopolitan city, where one doesn't judge a book by its cover. That mild-mannered, khaki-garbed, outdoor-type gentleman standing next to you in the grocery checkout line could pass for someone's gardener - but knowledgeable Orlandoans know that he is a citrus millionaire many times over, a graduate of a great university, a world traveler, and a valued supporter of many worthwhile projects, including the Symphony.

There are old-time residents and new residents, and each appreciates what the other has to offer. All who like our way of life and want to take part in it are welcome. It has always been that way.

Every city is unique because of its composition, its location, its climate, its history, its people. And its neighbors. Orlando's neighbors through the years have been among its greatest assets. Because of its size and accessibility, it is natural for Orlando to attract people from the surrounding area to shop for merchandise not carried in their own stores; to consult medical specialists and enter hospitals with specialized equipment; to transact banking and legal business; and to satisfy their own particular needs.

One of our neighbors' primary interests in coming to Orlando is the exceptional advantage of Orlando's cultural offerings. Among these are the art museums, the planetarium, musical and dramatic artists, touring Broadway shows, and groups brought in for concert, plus fine musicals and dramatic plays presented locally at the Civic Theatre and elsewhere.

More and more, as the years go by, people come from surrounding towns to the season of concerts given by the Florida Symphony Orchestra, with its nationally-known conductors and musicians, and the frequent appearance of renowned guest artists.

Especially supportive of cultural events in Orlando are the residents of our nearest neighbor, Winter Park, and Orlando reciprocates by its support of Winter Park events. We are as proud of Rollins College as they are, and praise the contributions this distinguished institution has made through its learned faculty, its educational offerings, its many cultural attractions. Because those in the news are usually intellectually oriented, Winter Park has gained the reputation of being 'high-brow.' It has its share of scholarly and highly-educated citizens, of course, but - like other cities, including Orlando - there's a good leavening of substantial citizens with business interests.

The Florida Symphony Orchestra is particularly grateful for the long-time support of Winter Park music lovers. They are faithful concert supporters, and their number grows each year. They fill the special buses which conveniently deposit them at the concert door, and pick them up when the concert is over. Many come in their own cars, of course, but the bus service makes it possible for older people and those who do not wish to drive at night to have safe and convenient transportation.

Although Rollins College is the oldest four-year and graduate college in the area, the state university system's Florida Technological University, and two fine community colleges - Valencia and Seminole - are also enthusiastic supporters of the Symphony.

Two other 'neighbors' deserve special mention: first, the Daytona Beach Symphony Society. Organized in 1952, this group has, from that date to this, presented the Florida Symphony Orchestra every winter in their own city - first with a five-concert season, and presently with a six-concert series. The caliber of guest artists they have chosen through the years is outstanding. Isaac Stern and Jan Peerce appeared their first season, Richard Tucker and Robert Merrill appeared in 1974, and the choices were comparable through all the intervening years. One of the Daytona Beach Symphony Society's biggest assets is its

Women's Guild, whose tireless efforts in support of 'their orchestra' have been magnificent.

The second 'special' neighbor is the home of the very first 'out-of-town' concert ever presented by the Florida Symphony - beautiful Mount Dora. SInce that first concert in 1952, Mount Dora has never wavered in its support of the orchestra. The Women's Committee of Mount Dora, formed only last season, is the Symphony's newest supporting organization, and well on its way to being the busiest. With a membership of over 100, and growing, the group is working now on plans and projects for 1975-76 and beyond.

Robert Frost wrote that "Good Fences Make Good Neighbors", but we might update that by saying "Good Music Makes Good Neighbors"; or, better yet, that "Good Neighbors Make Good Music". The Florida Symphony is confident that more and more good neighbors will join their friends in supporting Symphony concerts by their presence, by their enjoyment, and by their contributions.

The budget of the Florida Symphony Orchestra in its first season, 1950, was $30,000. Full professional status was achieved in 1953, making our orchestra the first all-professional orchestra in Florida. In its Silver Anniversary season, the orchestra's budget stands slightly in excess of $628,000. As the saying goes, "You've come a long way, baby." The 1974-75 season is 25 weeks in length, during which time over 80 concerts will be presented for audiences from Miami to Tallahassee - a rather remarkable advance from the six concerts of 1950's eight-week season.

Approximately 89 percent of the Florida Symphony's budget monies remain right here in Central Florida, in the form of orchestra salaries, payroll taxes, administrative and travel expenses, auditorium and office rental, supplies, and so on. Seventy cents out of every dollar goes to the orchestra salaries. A splendid regional orchestra of the quality of the Florida Symphony must have the finest professional musicians, and such musicians demand - and deserve - salaries commensurate with their abilities.

The Florida Symphony season includes musical fare of all types: Subscription Series concerts, youth concerts, POPS concerts,children's concerts, grand opera, ballet, and presentations with chorus. Spearheading active musical involvement are the members of the Board of Directors of the Florida Symphony Society, Inc., and the three 'Arms' of the Symphony - the Women's Committee, Associate Board, and Opera Gala Guild. Through their various projects they have made the Florida Symphony the cornerstone in the cultural lives of nearly a million Central Florida residents.

It is hard for the uninitiated to understand why box office receipts

8

are only a small part [actually, 17% in the case of the Florida Symphony] of the budget necessary to support a first-class Symphony Orchestra. When the Florida Symphony Society, Inc., ends a season 'in the black' it is a matter for national headlines. Few Symphonies ever enjoy that beatific state. It takes superb management and superhuman dedication to keep going. Fortunately, for 25 years, the Florida Symphony Orchestra has had such dedicated management.

In 1965, the Florida Symphony was one of sixty-one successful recipients among 200 applicants for a Ford Foundation Matching Grant, which provided $500,000 in endowment funds under the following conditions:

[1] that by June 30, 1971, the $500,000 be matched by community-raised funds;

[2] that these funds be placed in trust until June 1976, with only the income available to the Symphony until that time; and

[3] that the Orchestra continue to raise its annual operating funds as it had done in the past, while at the same time making every effort to expand activities, increase services, and improve the quality of the orchestra.

While the $500,000 was matched - the result of an unprecedented surge of community support - under the terms of the Grant, the orchestra must still raise its annual budget amount from the communities it serves. And since efforts to expand activities, increase services, and improve the quality of the orchestra have been successful beyond belief, the size of the yearly budget keeps growing like Topsy.

Since only $441,000 of 1974-75's $628,000 budget can possibly be realized from ticket sales, out-of-town concert revenue, grants from various governmental institutions, Trust income, program ads, PESO, and assistance from the Arms of the Symphony, the sizeable $187,000 balance is definitely a matter of community concern. In a sense, it is a matter of circular economy. Since, as previously stated, approximately 89 percent of the total budget remains in Central Florida, "The music [money] goes round and round", and most of it comes back home.

We welcome all the residents who have come to our area in recent years - many, no doubt, influenced by the cultural climate to be found here. We invite the new population to be a major factor in the growth of the Florida Symphony. The fact that such an acclaimed Symphony Orchestra has been able not only to survive, but, in WIlliam Faulkner's words, "to prevail", assures us that the long-time residents will continue their valued support. However, donations must rise in proportion to the area's population rise if the ever-widening gap between revenues and expenditures is to be bridged.

FORERUNNERS
OF
THE FLORIDA SYMPHONY

"The Mendelssohn Club" of around 1915, photographed at the Grand Theatre on West Pine Street. The gentleman standing at left of center front is Forrest Dabney Carr, Director. The mustachioed gentleman beside him is Rev. Gray, at that time Orlando's Episcopal minister, and popular bass soloist.

When Orlando was young - from its first settlement in the 1860's, through the Gay Nineties and the Edwardian years of the early part of the 20th Century - it was settled by pioneers of many different backgrounds. There were the Indian fighters, the often shrewd though perhaps unschooled homesteaders from other states, intent on making a new home for their families - and there were the rascals and adventurers, fleeing from misadventures elsewhere.

There was, curiously, still another type of settler - one who had quite a sophisticated background of education and experience, and came to Florida for its salubrious climate, its tropical beauty, and the bonus - a very favorable chance of capitalizing on these assets and making a fortune. It was an odd combination of cultures, yet it produced a most interesting amalgam whereby each profited from the qualities of the other.

Did you know that the Orlando of early days had a well-patronized Opera House in 1883? It was located on the east side of Court Street in what is now downtown Orlando. "Something for everyone", was its program. The Opera House hosted skating parties, spelling bees, auctions, religious services, church suppers, as well as balls, lectures, Chautauqua series, plays, and musicales. Everybody came - it was the only game in town! Seated among the world-traveled dowagers and their husbands, living on inherited wealth, the Gay Blades of the polo set [oh yes, Orlando had polo matches and horse races and golf courses then] were the Florida backwoodsmen and their families. Even as you and I, these parents yearned for a more advantaged life for their families than they themselves had had.

There was an Orlando Concert Band, organized in 1886. Their very good music was a popular addition to Orlando's life, and to other communities to which they were invited. Their handsome, brass-buttoned, braid-trimmed uniforms made them a stand-out wherever they appeared in the state.

Among early Orlando residents were Dr. and Mrs. P. Phillips, a widely-traveled and cultured couple. Dr. Phillips owned a great deal of land in Florida and had extensive citrus interests. Around 1910 he backed Mr. Walter Drennen in presenting a series of concerts in the well-appointed new Lucerne Theatre. Artists appearing in these

Dr. P. Phillips

Della [Mrs. P.] Phillips   Ina McReynolds

12

concerts included such celebrated musical stars as Mischa Elman, Josef Hofmann, the Letz String Quartet, Frieda Hempel, and Lotte Lehmann.

In 1909, Mr. Drennen - a fine musician - had organized a group of local musicians into "The Mendelssohn Club". Their avowed aim was pretty high-sounding: "The advancement of musical art in Orlando, and to develop the talent and stimulate interest in music among its members." Men and women members enthusiastically rehearsed once a week, and soon were ready for public performances. Under the direction of Walter Drennen, Walter Steacy Holmes, and Forrest Dabney Carr, they gave monthly concerts and also presented such Gilbert and Sullivan light operas as H.M.S. PINAFORE and THE MIKADO. Mrs. Braxton Beacham was accompanist for the club's performances and remembers that their first performance was a contata, "The Rose Maiden". Among members were those whose names are still familiar and prominent in Orlando business and social life: the Beardalls, Cheneys, Guernseys, Harry Voorhis, Cestie Lawton, and others. On the crest of the cultural wave, Dr. Phillips built the Phillips Theatre at Pine Street and Orange Avenue, completed in 1917. At that time, it had the finest facilities the area had ever seen.

Soon after World War I, Dr. and Mrs. Phillips began giving afternoon and evening concerts in their home. Guests were invited to hear such famous artists as Metropolitan opera star Evelyn Scotney, violinist Eddie Brown, the Letz Quartet and others. Dr. Phillips, music lover that he was, had a pipe organ in his home, and, although he admitted that he played the violin as a rank amateur, he had a professional's knowledge of antique violins and owned a priceless collection of them.

> Sentimentally I am disposed to harmony,
>   but organically
> I am incapable of a tune.
>
> — Charles Lamb

An old program reveals that there was an Orlando Symphony Orchestra, alive and flourishing, organized in 1924 - fifty years ago - which could well give rise to the happy idea that we might well celebrate a fiftieth anniversary this year, as well as a 25th. Edgar Atholburt Ball was conductor of that symphony orchestra, programs were held in Memorial High School Auditorium, Orrin Robinson was President of the organization, and Frank W. Reed was Business

Manager. Mrs. W. J. Morrison was chairman of the Committee, Mrs. G. E. Krug was Vice-chairman, and A. T. Browning was treasurer.

Heading the long list of prominent Orlando and Winter Park citizens who were Symphony patrons a half-century ago was Dr. Mary Leonard. Judging from available records, Dr. Leonard took over the infant orchestra of 1924 and re-activated it - or perhaps founded a new one - who, now, can say? At any rate, in 1926-27 her orchestra became quite active and continued so during the depression years. She remained its incomparable manager through all the difficult years until her death in New York City in October, 1940.

In 1941, after Dr. Leonard's death during the previous October, George C. Keiser became president of the Symphony Orchestra of Central Florida; Mrs. A. E. Dick was first vice-president, Mrs. Leonard Dyer, 2nd vice-president, Miss Matilda Campbell, secretary, Henry Schenck, treasurer, and Board members were Dean Winslow S. Anderson, of Rollins College, Mrs. Irving Bacheller, Mrs. E. S. Fownes, Mrs. McCullough Maguire and Mrs. Tracy Lay.

The entire community took great pride in the fine concerts the Symphony Orchestra of Central Florida had given in its off again-on again sixteen years of existence, frequently under great difficulties. Everybody had helped. The great Metropolitan Opera star, Louise Homer, had retired with her husband, composer Sidney Homer, to Winter Park. Madame Homer had seven operatic pupils, and for the Memorial Concert to the late Dr. Leonard in February, 1941, these young singers presented two of Sidney Homer's well-known songs, "Requiem", and "There's Heaven Above." The late Dr. Hamilton Holt, then President of Rollins College, eulogized Dr. Mary Leonard in these words:

"Her loss would be irreparable did we not know that one's best efforts enter into the permanent assets of the community and thus never die."

Dr. Rhea Marsh Smith, then a young Rollins College faculty professor, and later head of the History Department, remembers rowing a canoe across Lake Osceola to sit on the spacious lawn of the Brewer Estate with other music lovers, while the orchestra played. The estate gardens were filled with exotic botanical treasures brought from all over the world, so it was a special treat to go there for concerts. The Symphony also played in the old Rec Hall on the Rollins Campus.

Dr. Leonard was a resourceful administrator. The musicians for the orchestra had been recruited by her from the community, and were happy to donate their talents. Many of them, in those Depression days, had had to give up their music profession and take any job they could find. Some carpenters, plumbers, and workers in many other

Dr. Mary Leonard

labor fields were now playing the music they loved with special verve, and revived memories of happier times. Some had ties with well-known artists, and could help in securing them as guest artists with the symphony.

One of Dr. Leonard's greatest accomplishments was in persuading Dr. Alexander Bloch, then head of the Music Department of Rollins College, to serve as director of the orchestra. Bloch was well-known in Europe, as well as America, for his talents as violinist, composer and conductor. He had studied in Leningrad under Leopold Auer, one of the world's foremost violin teachers. For some time, Bloch was Auer's first assistant teacher. Heifitz, Zimbalist, Elman, Seidl and Kathleen Parlow are a few of Auer's famous pupils.

After his return to America, Bloch served as guest conductor of the NBC Symphony in New York, and the National Symphony Orchestra in Washington, D. C.

Dr. Bloch continued his service as conductor of the Symphony Orchestra of Central Florida into the early 1940s, but by 1943, with all the disruptions of World War II - with musicians, like everyone else, being called to service, or to some other phase of the tremendous war effort - the orchestra was compelled to become inactive. By this time, Dr. Bloch, because of ill health, had retired to his winter home on Sarasota's Siesta Key. The great conductor and his wife, Mrs. Blanche Bloch, who had given delightful lecture-musicals the evening before each concert, were greatly missed in Central Florida.

A few years later, when Dr. Bloch's health improved, he became conductor of the fledgling Florida West Coast Symphony, where he guided and shaped the orchestra for eleven years, significantly affecting the cultural growth of the entire Sarasota-Bradenton area.

At the end of the 1961 season, Dr. Bloch retired for the second time. "My doctor frowns at the idea of an 80-year-old man with a heart condition standing up and waving his arms for two hours", he said.

When Dr. Bloch was 79, he came back to Orlando to conduct the Florida Symphony in one of his own compositions, and his many friends in the audience gave him a standing ovation. Among them were two popular local guest artists from Bloch's conducting years in Orlando — pianists Jesse Pedrick Baker and Dorothy Morton Parks. Now in his nineties, Dr. Bloch is still composing, teaching on a limited scale, and attending occasional concerts.

After the war, in 1946-47, the Symphony Board hoped to be able to reassemble and reorganize the Symphony Orchestra of Central Florida, and in an effort to do so, planned three benefit concerts to raise money. The first concert, on February 1, 1947, featured the Gordon String Quartet; the second, on March 5, presented the duo-piano team of Braggiotti and Chaikin; and the final concert, on March 14, presented the great Metropolitan baritone, Lawrence Tibbett. These concerts were successful, but more support was needed if the symphony was to regain its previous standing.

The area was not without music, of course. The Rollins Chamber Orchestra, under the direction of Christopher O. Honaas, gave a number of concerts. One, in April, 1948, given at the Winter Park Woman's Club, received much praise. It featured Bach's great Brandenburg Concerto, plus selections by Mozart, Vivaldi, Beethoven, and Samuel Barber's "Dover Beach", for which Edward Langley was the baritone soloist.

In rapid retrospect, an 'Orlando Symphony Orchestra' was formed in 1924, and by the 1930's it had expanded into a group called the 'Central Florida Symphony Orchestra.' It was composed of from forty to fifty amateur musicians. World War II caused cessation of activities - and shortly after that is where our narrative begins in earnest.

But what a musical heritage the Florida Symphony Orchestra has!

An Opera House as far back as 1883 . . .

A concert band in 1886, with brass buttons, yet . . .

A constellation of brilliant guest artists for Walter Drennen's concerts, with backing by Dr. P. Phillips . . .

The home concerts given by Dr. and Mrs. P. Phillips, with famous musicians performing for the guests . . .

The well-remembered Mendelssohn Club, whose young men and women members had a wonderful time giving concerts and presenting Gilbert & Sullivan operettas to delighted audiences . . .

Dr. Mary Leonard's Symphony Orchestra of Central Florida, in Winter Park . . .

The Central Florida Symphony Orchestra, in Orlando.

By the late 1940's, this part of Florida was already converted, and its citizens were true believers in the necessity for a Symphony Orchestra for any community that wanted its citizens to enjoy the finer things of life.

> *Knowing is not enough;*
> *we must apply.*
> *Willing is not enough;*
> *we must do.*
>
> — *Goethe*

So, in 1950, when a group of music lovers decided to organize a Central Florida Symphony Society to explore possibilities [it later

17

became the Florida Symphony Society when, wonder of wonders, our grasp really did exceed our reach], some people thought it would be a breeze to support a symphony orchestra . . . nothing to it! These people just didn't know the score, as we say in musical circles. They had never tried to organize and keep a fine symphony orchestra solvent and growing. Well, happily - twenty-five years later we're still solvent [sort of!], and growing like crazy!

Fortunately, along with the happy optimists, there were a number of hardheaded skeptics, who did know what a great task it would be, but - contrary to their nature - were willing to try it, anyway. Because they loved music.

We will trace the progress of this ambitious group. They could never admit being tired. They could never give up. They convinced themselves, against all odds, that there was no such thing as an impossible dream, and they kept drawing on limitless stores of faith and energy, their only requirement being that it must be done to the sound of music.

First Rollins Orchestra, pictured in 1911. Susan Dyer, Director. L to R: Top Row: Gus Moreman,* Andy Ahik, Dike Witherell, Miss Daniels, Susan Dyer, Watson Moreman, Girard Denning. Front Row, L to R: Miss Daniels, Miss Nehrling, Berta Smith Schultz, Mrs. F. W. [Martha] Shepherd*, Ray Trovillion *.

[* surviving members.]

18

THE FRENCH CONNECTION

"If we could have devised an arrangement for providing everybody with music in their homes, perfect in quality, and beginning and ceasing at will, we should have considered the limit of human felicity already attained."

— *Edward Bellamy*

Yves Chardon

"Be favorable to bold beginnings."

— Virgil

World War II brought changes to Central Florida. After the restrictions and shortages of the war years, there was now a comparative abundance of merchandise, building materials for new business establishments and homes, and a general desire to put the anxieties and austerities of the war years behind and get on with the good life everyone felt was needed and deserved.

The population had grown - defense plants, Air Force installations, nearby space flights in the making, and growing interest in Florida as a land of opportunity had brought many new residents to the area. Some were quick-money seekers, of course, but many were substantial citizens ready to do their part in promoting the orderly growth of their newly-adopted homeland.

Such growth included not only bread-and-butter necessities, but new highways, an expanded and enriched school system, playgrounds, sports and recreation facilities, and - entertainment! The entertainment most desired was not the honky-tonk, X-rated variety, but good family entertainment. Newcomers were glad to hear of cultural events offered, and particularly glad to hear of plans for reactivation of the former Central Florida Symphony Orchestra.

No one seems to remember all of the people who got down to the business of reorganization. One who spearheaded the move, however, was John Tiedtke, then newly-appointed as Treasurer of Rollins College. John called the old board to his office to try to get the orchestra going again. He recalls that Jessica Dyer, especially, was bursting with enthusiasm — and a few weeks later, she had found the man to head the effort: Robert S. Carr. He was the one, in those days, who was the first to be called upon when there was a hard job to be done. He was the one who could see the pitfalls, but knew ways to climb out of financial morasses. Bob Carr also had the vision to glimpse the rainbow beyond all the dark clouds. He had previously - and successfully - headed innumerable charity drives, war bond drives, and civic betterment projects. He had been Mayor of Orlando for several terms, and knew people all over the country to whom he could turn

20

for information and advice. Bob Carr accepted the presidency of the new Central Florida Symphony Society, and on May 21, 1950, called together a small group of interested citizens to make plans for the revitalization and reorganization of the former symphony nucleus.

Others there were probably Miss Rose Phelps, philanthropist and music lover; Mrs. Leonard Dyer, of Winter Park, familiar with great orchestras in Europe and America; Miss Helen Ryan and Miss Joy Hawley, co-owners of the elegant 'Whistling Oyster Gift Shops' in Orlando and Ogunquit, Maine, who not only had business acumen but great musical interest and promotional ability; Dr. A. H. Spivack, a doctor by profession but a life-long music lover; and Dr. Kenneth Steady, a chiropractor, professionally, but a 'cellist, artistically. And there were others.

They elected an excellent Board. And the Board had immediate problems. Where would they get the money for a symphony orchestra which was not even in existence at that time? Where could they find volunteer musicians for the time being? What would arouse musical interest in people whose intent was riveted on building houses, and streets, and subdivisions and new businesses - or on resuming the professions and jobs they had left for war activities?

They knew they must find a conductor of great talent and prestige in order to launch the new symphony successfully. Luckily, they soon found one who lived up to all their qualifications; Yves Chardon.

Maestro Chardon, it was learned, was "in the neighborhood." He had been a guest conductor for a series of concerts with the Havana [Cuba] Symphony Orchestra, and agreed to come by Orlando to discuss the plans here. He was interested. All of his life he had been a man who welcomed challenge, and it would be a milestone in his distinguished career to start with comparatively raw material and bring forth symphonic greatness. He was introduced to important people, including musical personages of the faculties of Stetson University, DeLand, and Rollins College, Winter Park. His attention was disarmingly directed to the verdant countryside, the beauty of the surroundings, the pleasant climate.

Madame Chardon [Henriette de Constant], having just completed a concert tour with the Minneapolis Symphony which she vowed - in her charming French accent - was 'from one blizzard to another', basked in the sunshine. The Symphony hosts knew that they had won.

Yves Chardon had an impressive background. He was a graduate of the Paris Conservatory of Music, and was considered the leading 'Cellist in France by the time he was 15 years old. When he was 22, he had his own orchestra in France. At the age of 25, the young artist was tempted, by Dr. Serge Koussevitsky, to come to the New World as a member of Koussevitsky's Boston Symphony. Chardon came to the United States in 1929, and was joined soon afterward by his wife, also a concert 'Cellist.

During his 14 years in Boston with Koussevitsky, Chardon organized the Chardon String Quartet and became widely known throughout the East. He headed the professional orchestra department of the Longy School, Cambridge, Massachusetts, one of the country's outstanding schools of music, and an affiliate of the Eccle Normal, in Paris. In 1944, Chardon accpeted the post of associate conductor of the Minneapolis Symphony, with Dimitri Mitropoulos.

In 1948, Chardon was presented the highest cultural award of the French government — the Officier de L' Instruction Publique — for his achievements in music. In 1949, in Paris, he conducted the season's first concert with the Societe des Concerts du Conservatoire. Following the 1949 concert season in Minneapolis, he conducted concerts of the Havana Symphony, from whence Orlando persuaded him to come here to consider the musical directorship of the Central Florida Symphony Orchestra.

Once a distinguished conductor had been captivated, musicians for the orchestra had to be found. It was hoped that some of the very best professional musicians, ready for their retirement from great orchestras, might have come to Florida for their later years — and might be willing to play for less money than they had received during their active careers. These professional musicians would be used to help train each portion of the orchestra. And so it was! There were, in addition to retired professional musicians, plentiful reservoirs of talent: Stetson University in DeLand, Rollins College in Winter Park, musicians from the former Symphony Orchestra of Central Florida founded by Dr. Mary Leonard, most of whom had gone on to form the Central Florida Symphony Orchestra in Orlando. From this ecumenical group, some 40 musicians were gathered to form a Central Florida Symphony Orchestra, to present a test concert directed by Chardon.

It is not surprising that Chardon was dismayed at the beginning. He was confronted with an orchestra comprised of fifteen trumpets, twenty saxophones, dozens of drums, and a very few strings, all enthusiastically gathered to practice for the first time. He looked on in horror. He had wanted to play Beethoven's "Egmont Overture" at the first concert, and he must have wondered how many of this group had ever even heard of it. But Chardon was not only a musician of the first rank, he was also a hard worker. "We must have the best orchestra in Florida", he said. "It is a necessity, a question of survival, for our winter audiences are accustomed to the top orchestras of the nation."

The busy months that followed that May 21, 1950 organizational

22

meeting of the Central Florida Symphony Society are remembered with bemused amazement by those who blithely undertook this project. "Did we really do all of that?", they ask each other now. Recruiting musicians, planning programs, wining and dining possible patrons, selling tickets, fund raising, publicity — there was never a dull moment.

The newspapers were generous concerning every activity. Chardon always had a good press. The Paris papers had noted about his French appearances, "His success has been overwhelming." In Minneapolis, the reviews spoke of his musicianship: "He achieved vocal smoothness and beauty of phrase seldom heard from any orchestra." The Havana papers wrote of "Finesse of detail, orchestral clarity, poetic intention and lyricism", and — not to be outdone — the Orlando papers complimented Yves Chardon with such phrases as "Can make music come to vibrant life. Amazing conductor. The conductor led the Beethoven Pastoral Symphony with his usual impeccable tempi, maintaining a brisk clip in the refreshing allegro of the third and fourth movements without falling into a metronome beat."

Robert Craig, who served the Symphony Society a brief time as business manager, had his hands full keeping up with the many activities. Arrangements were made for concerts for the schools. Chamber music sections of the Orchestra played for special afternoon, evening and dinner programs. Phil Spitalny's All-Girl Orchestra appeared under the auspices of the Symphony Society in the fall, and shared the proceeds, as one of the initial money-raising events. Arrangements were made for special buses to transport concert-goers from Winter Park to Orlando for any and all symphony events.

Did they forget anything? Perhaps so, but they certainly tried to touch all bases to insure that the first real concert of the Central Florida Symphony Orchestra, in January, 1951, would be long-remembered in the cultural life of Central Florida.

That first concert was held on January 5, 1951, in Orlando Municipal Auditorium. It was a stirring and bravura performance, which brought a near-capacity audience to its feet, shouting and applauding.

> *Beetheoven's Fifth Symphony is the*
> *most sublime noise that has*
> *ever penetrated into the ear of man.*
>
> — *Edward Morgan Forster*

Already, it seemed, Yves Chardon had brought his musicians, gathered from such diverse fields, into a melodic and unified whole

23

that responded to his inspired direction and his interpretations — skillfully, beautifully, and willingly. This was not an easy program — Weber's "Euryanthe" Overture, Beethoven's "Fifth Symphony", Walter Piston's "Concerto for Orchestra", with its curiously ingratiating dissonances and difficult modern rhythms. The final number was the masterful "Capriccio Espagnol" of Rimsky-Korsakov, which one critic has called "the soul of Spain in a Slavic mold."

Not only was the audience critically listening to a new Orchestra, but to a new Director, and they expressed their satisfaction with both. Chardon had demonstrated that he was equally at home with the classical and the modern in orchestral music, and that he could impart his knowledge to his musicians. In this he was aided by Dr. Kenneth Steady, who was the assistant conductor.

Finances notwithstanding, it was decided that the Orchestra should have a Pops Concert series in the future. Reasoning was that this was a good way to introduce good music — including the lighter classics, — to the public, at popular prices, and at the same time motivate Pops audiences to support the whole Symphony program.

With their "Why not now?" spirit, the Board set up the first Pops Concert on March 15, 1951. Percy Grainger, famed pianist and composer, was the guest artist. One of his piano offerings with the Orchestra was the Edvard Grieg Piano Concerto. Grainger and Grieg were long-time friends, and he always included many Grieg compositions in his concerts. Grieg was so enthusiastic over Grainger's playing that he noted in his diary: "Yes, he is a genius. That is sure enough. I have never met anyone who understands me as he does." The audience thoroughly enjoyed this Pops Concert, and were especially pleased that Grainger had incleued two familiar pieces of his own composition, "Country Gardens", and "Shepherds Hey".

During the first season, the first guests to appear with the Symphony were three local pianists — Helen Moore, Jesse Pedrick Baker, and Manly Duckworth.

Another guest artist was a 15-year-old Cuban musical prodigy who had impressed Chardon when he was conducting the Havana Symphony. Nenita Escandon played Beethoven's "Third Piano Concerto in C Minor" for the third concert of the 1950-51 season.

Chardon's wife, Henriette de Constant, held the position of Principal 'Cellist in her husband's orchestra. She was also a moving spirit in the growing chamber-music activities in Orlando and Winter Park. She was 'Cello soloist for Saint-Saens' "Cello Concerto in A Minor, Opus 33", during the fifth concert of the first season. On the same program, Vivaldi's "La Primavera" [Spring], from "The Four Seasons", featured violin solos by Alphonse Carlo, Concertmaster, Gustav Kleiner, and

Alice Sager, of the orchestra's ensemble group, plus the piano artistry of Katherine Carlo, and an organ solo by Jesse Pedrick Baker.

Music is often called the language of the emotions.
— *Charles O'Connell*

The Chardons were an interesting addition to Orlando society. With their sophisticated Gallic charm, their delightful French accents, and obvious mastery of their art, their presence was a new experience for many Floridians. Both Chardons were temperamental, which was not surprising, but they also had wide differences of opinion, personally. Mrs. Chardon was a member of a titled French family, while Maestro Chardon was not. Both were 'cellists of concert quality, but there, too, they had differences of opinion as to technique and interpretation. Henriette de Constant's brother, Baron Paul d'Estournelle, was head of the French Studies at Rollins College for a time, and there was 'talk' in Winter Park when the Baron and a glamorous socialite left town at the same time, leaving behind her husband and his beauteous young wife, the Baroness — who, it is said, now lives in California. Presently, the lady in the case has long been married to a well-known entrepreneur of music productions in New York and Salzburg, Austria. The Baron died very soon after leaving Florida.

It was something of a miracle that Chardon was able to bring order out of the chaos of the original 'orchestra' gathered for his approval. He was a superb musician, but he was not tolerant of inattention, amateurism, or mediocrity. Several things are recalled which happened during his tenure as conductor.

A member of the original group, Charlie Goldberg, who played both violin and cymbals [amazingly enough], also had the librarian's assignment of arranging the music for the orchestra. This he did at home, and came early to rehearsals to distribute parts to musicians. No doubt he hurried through his various tasks, and when he assumed his place to play, was breathless. One night, he not only came in ahead of time with his one magnificent cymbal crash! — but, to add insult to injury, in the first movement of a Brahms Symphony, the cymbal strap broke and the cymbal flew through the air — falling to earth, we know not where. If looks could kill!

Another time, a snare drummer encountered a work requiring him to play the same sequence over and over, so that he became almost mesmerized and lost his place. As a consequence, he and his drums continued 'rolling' after the music stopped. His head very likely rolled shortly thereafter.

Chardon's wrath was mighty, but it really climaxed once in Mount Dora when a little old violinist [who had been an excellent performer at one time, before his hearing and eyesight began to fail] was having trouble with a dazzling Prokofiev opus. Suddenly the Maestro's nerves could stand it no longer, and he came at the unfortunate violinist, screaming: "You are fired! Get out!"

All six subscription concerts that first season were well-chosen and musically demanding. Chardon was never able to reconcile himself to an inexperienced orchestra. He chose the most difficult music, and since he was accustomed to great orchestras with highly-professional training, he sometimes forgot and decided to change the order of the numbers suddenly. This would throw the musicians into a panic, as they scrambled to get the proper music ready. Chardon was an inspiring conductor, though, and the orchestra was complimented that he had such confidence in them, so they responded amazingly well.

Though the budget that first season was only $30,000, covering conductor's salary, a small stipend for a few key musicians, hall rental, music purchase, and the like — still, even those few dollars were hard to come by. Most fortunately, the orchestra had an anonymous guardian angel, who would telephone President Bob Carr each week to ask how much was needed to meet expenses. Carr, an expert at figures, bridge, symphonic music, and touching people for donations for worthwhile projects, knew each time to the the exact penny. The next morning, a check would be on his desk to take care of the Symphony for another week. Secrecy was the order, along with the check, and though some in position to know suspected who the generous donor was, the name has never been officially revealed.

The fact that the orchestra was giving free concerts for school children, and that servicemen had been given free tickets to subscription series concerts, made a highly favorable impression on the general public. The whole first season had been successful beyond anyone's wildest dreams, and the Board was determined that there could be no let down. So much accomplished — so much yet to do! And so, through the long, hot summer of 1951, plans were made for the orchestra's second season — and beyond.

The Symphony's program for the second season included six subscription concerts and a number of extras. Yves Chardon was fast becoming Florida's most talked-about and written-about celebrity for his success in bringing a new orchestra to smooth and brilliant

26

performance. Though he was temperamental and autocratic, exceedingly demanding and not very tactful, he was very artistic and an inspired conductor. Chardon was ambitious and hard-working. He was really determined to make this orchestra the finest in Florida. To that end, he planned a tour so that the orchestra would become well-known throughout the state and even beyond.

The tour of the Southeastern states started in Gainesville, Florida, and progressed to Raleigh, High Point and Asheville, N.C.; Greenville and Spartanburg, S.C.; and Augusta and Athens, Ga. The tour lasted over a week, and the orchestra played a different place every day — or night, as the case might be. Helen Traubel, the great Wagnerian soprano, was the guest artist for all except the concluding performance in Augusta, at which time the Brahms Double Concerto for violin and 'cello was performed by Alphonse Carlo and Henriette de Constant.

Miss Rose Phelps, a generous angel of the symphony from the beginning, accompanied the orchestra on this tour, and they really appreciated her always confident and happy disposition [and generous expense money] when the going got tough. For they did have adventures.

For instance, when they were ready to leave Gainesville, it was found that the driver of the truck hauling the instruments was dead drunk. Chardon, who always seemed to live in another world [which mortals could only glimpse] and who disdained such practical matters as carrying money in his pockets, could rise to an occasion, when necessary. The Maestro got behind the wheel of the truck and drove it, himself, to the next stop! Most of the others had preceded him, and were not at all sure he would arrive, or — having arrived — find them — but he did! To coin a phrase, 'cherchez les musicians.'

Another near-disaster concerned a hotel scene that might have come right out of the Old West. It seems that the day before the orchestra arrived in Augusta, was pay day at a nearby Army base. Predictably, the town was full of soldiers looking for hotel accomodations as well as excitement. Mrs. Chardon had gone to her room to rest, and to practice quietly on her 'cello for her guest appearance that night. Suddenly there came a loud knocking on her door. When she answered it, she discovered a soldier, slightly the worse for wear, who tearfully asked if he could come in and listen to the beautiful music. Others nearby were interested, too, including [so they heard, later] the heavyweight champion of Georgia. Madame Chardon was beside herself with indignation, and in a fine mixture of French and English called for the manager, the police, and anyone else who could get these unwelcome admirers away from her door. Finally, things got settled down, leaving only a non-functioning shower head in the bath to disturb Madame's composure. The surprising Yves Chardon was equal to this, too, and managed to repair the shower, although he tore his tuxedo coat in the process. It was, nevertheless, a successful tour. In any event, everybody said so!

In the early spring of 1952, the Central Florida Symphony Orchestra gave a concert in Miami, and the Miami newspapers were prodigal with praise for Chardon and his musicians. It was during this season, also, that the Central Florida Symphony Society and the newly-organized Daytona Beach Symphony Society formed a collaboration by which the orchestra would present a series of concerts in Daytona Beach each season — an association which has continued without interruption from that day to this.

Because of many commitments, Robert S. Carr only kept the presidency of the Symphony Society during its first crucial year of reorganization. His place was filled by the election of John G. Baker, prominent Orlando attorney, as the group's second president.

The expanded program of the symphony in its second bona fide season required a larger budget, and in late October, 1951, some 200 women of the area got together at the San Juan Hotel to plan a mammoth fund-raising drive. Mrs. A. H. Smith, Jr., was general chairman. It was decided that they would try, in one intensive week of hard work, to raise the money needed for the coming season. The communites responded handsomely, and the results of this drive were satisfying not only in the money raised, but in the increased interest in the symphony throughout the area.

The first Youth Concert by the Central Florida Symphony Orchestra was given Saturday afternoon, January 26, 1952 in the Orlando Municipal Auditorium. Mrs. Jeannette Hogue, music supervisor of Orange County schools, was in charge. Buses brought students from Tavares, Leesburg, Eustis and Mount Dora, in Lake County; from Sanford, in Seminole County; and from Kissimmee in Osceola County. Members of the Orlando Senior High School bands assisted in the ticket office and at the doors.

Having seen what enthusiastic women could do in fund-raising, the Symphony Board decided it was time for a permanent, on-going Women's Committee to be organized. Little sooner said than done, in February of 1952 Mrs. Loomis C. Leedy was named the first president of the new Women's Committee. She and her group immediately started plans for helping the orchestra in many ways, and some of their efforts will be noted in their story under the ARMS OF THE SYMPHONY chapter.

By the end of the orchestra's second season, Chardon insisted that — in view of what they had accomplished, and the evident approval of the large audiences — all his musicians should be paid. Everyone agreed. So it came to pass that beginning with the 1952-53 season, the Florida Symphony became the very first all-professional orchestra in the state. It was at this time, also, that the name of the orchestra was officially changed from the Central Florida Symphony to the Florida Symphony. This was considered appropriate, as it did not localize the orchestra, and recognized its greater scope as a state or regional orchestra.

As plans for the now fully-professional Florida Symphony's next season progressed, it became increasingly evident that money — as always — was a problem. Concertgoers, seeing the crowds who came to the concerts, could not understand why box office receipts would not be sufficient. Then, as now, they failed to realize that there are many added expenses that ticket sales simply cannot cover. Even when the infant symphony was at its peak of audience acceptance, with reviews praising the performances in the most glowing terms, and national media taking note of the orchestra's success, the Board of Directors knew that their funds were critically low.

But help came, in many ways, and from many quarters. On January 9, 1953, during a concert intermission, Florida's late U.S. Senator, Spessard Holland, spoke over a state-wide Columbia Broadcasting network, from Orlando, about the value of great music to a community. The program for the evening was broadcast over this same network, being heard in Jacksonville, St. Augustine, Miami, Fort Myers, Tampa, West Palm Beach, Sarasota, and all points in between.

29

Obviously, the Florida Symphony Orchestra, in its third season, was garnering more and more favorable national comment. Music critics of the Cleveland Plain Dealer, The Boston Globe, the New York Herald Tribune, and even Time Magazine, had taken note of this surprisingly successful young orchestra.

In August, 1953, Good Housekeeping Magazine's music editor, George Marek, published an article titled "Can You Afford An Orchestra of Your Own?", using the Florida Symphony as a glowing example. He wrote:

"The weather had already turned uncomfortably warm in Orlando, Florida, but the concert hall was densely crowded. At the end of the evening the audience of more than two thousand persons stood up and wildly cheered Bidu Sayao, the soloist, Yves Chardon, the conductor, and the musicians. A portion of this applause might well have been directed at the audience itself. They had reason to congratulate themselves. After three years, Orlando — a community of but 60,000 persons — had built a good and stable Symphony Orchestra — indeed, an exceptionally good one, which had been praised by such punctilious judges as Artur Rubinstein and Yehudi Menuhin."

The article went on to detail the many ways — scrambling or smoothly-functioning — in which the Florida Symphony backers had been able to achieve the success they were experiencing, and the promise of the future in the growing community.

One of the highlights of the 1952-53 season was the first ballet program presented by the symphony, with the cooperation of the Royal School of Dance. Both the orchestra and some forty Royal dancers contributed their talents, with proceeds going to Goodfellows, Inc.'s annual charity of providing food and toys for the needy at Christmas.

At the Symphony Society's annual meeting in April of 1953, Miss Helen Ryan was elected as the third president of the organization, a position which she held for seven years, subsequently becoming Executive Vice-President and General Manager for another dozen years. Under her guidance the Florida Symphony has accomplished the near-impossible, has grown, in both size and ability, has expanded its services, extended its season, and — survived. Perhaps 'thrived' is a better word.

The Junior League of Orlando gave the first Symphony Ball on February 10, 1954. It was a sumptuous affair, held in the beautifully-decorated Orlando Coliseum. The Florida Symphony presented a program, during which Maestro Chardon stepped down from the bandstand to waltz Miss Ryan around the room. Following the orchestra's program, Tony Perez and his dance band played for the festivities til the wee hours of the morning.

Jerome Hines, dramatic bass-baritone, made his initial appearance with the orchestra during the 1953-54 season. At the after-concert party, held at the home of Dr. and Mrs. Elwyn Evans, he shunned the party food [probably dieting, as he is a very large man], and shocked the housekeeper by going straight to the kitchen, cooking his own eggs, and squeezing two quarts of fine Temple orange juice, which he proceeded to consume on the spot.

In March of 1954 a second ballet concert was presented, with proceeds again going to charity. Dancers from the Ebsen School sparkled in excerpts from Tchaikovsky's "Swan Lake", as did the Royal dancers, who presented Offenbach's "Gaite Parisienne."

The 1954 season also included a unique evening, which began with a concert featuring both the Florida Symphony and the Florida Symphony Student Orchestra. Following this, musicians from the local union furnished music for dancing from ten 'til midnight! This is only one example of the outstanding support and cooperation which the American Federation of Musicians Local #389 has given to the symphony through the years.

Yves Chardon had done a most noteworthy task in molding the young orchestra into a cohesive unit, but at the end of the 1953-54 season he elected to abandon conductorial duties and return to performing as a 'cellist. He is presently with the Metropolitan Opera Orchestra in New York, and is also active in Chamber Music groups and as a composer.

The Chardons were divorced soon after leaving Orlando, and Henriette de Constant presently lives in Westport Point, Massachusetts, on a farm which is very European in character. The farmhouse is picturesque, reflecting its owner's taste in furniture and accessories. Florida friends who have visited Henriette remember well the gourmet meals she prepares, and speak of the unusual sight of that elegant small artist driving a Jeep as if she had always favored that mode of travel.

The Chardon children are grown up now. Christine is married to a successful advertising man, James Schneider, and they have two lovely children. Their home is in Birmingham, Michigan. Dr. Roland Chardon, the older son, is a geologist at the University of Miami [Florida] while Alain, the younger son, is a forestry specialist in New England.

L to R: Mrs. Authur Frentz, Yves Chardon, Artur Rubenstein, Henriette de Constant [Mrs. Chardon] and Harrison Hollander.

MUSIC: THE AMERICAN WAY
with FRANK MILLER

Frank Miller

When Frank Miller was signed to direct the Florida Symphony Orchestra in April, 1954, this big, tall, American conductor presented quite a change from the volatile, slender, French Chardon. Chardon had done a great job in molding the orchestra, and left quite a challenge to anyone who came after him. To compound this challenge, for Frank Miller, was the public's propensity for thinking that leadership in the arts must come from the Old World, and that Americans were leaders only in business and industry.

Frank Miller, however, in his quiet way, soon convinced Central Florida that he was equal to the task at hand. He was a 15-year veteran of the NBC Symphony Orchestra in New York, and former assistant conductor under Arturo Toscanini. Mr. Miller was first 'Cellist with the NBC Symphony, and had played with both the Philadelphia and the Minneapolis Symphonys. When Toscanini's retirement brought about the dissolution of the NBC Symphony, the great Maestro himself had recommended Frank Miller for the Florida Symphony post. To add to his credentials, Miller was also a member of the New York Piano Quartet which recorded under the Columbia label.

Soon after his tenure began in the fall of 1954, Miller organized a group called 'The Florida Symphony Orchestra Singers' to prepare for a production of "The Gondoliers," by Gilbert & Sullivan, on March 25-26, 1955. Miller had conducted more than a hundred performances of Gilbert & Sullivan light operas as a hobby, in his spare time, during his years with the NBC Symphony, so he approached his task with obvious relish. In Orlando, he set up rehearsals on Wednesday evening of each week, for all singers who were interested, and he soon had a fine group happily Gilbert & Sullivan-ing.

Things are seldom what they seem
  Skim milk masquerades as cream.
              Buttercup and Captain duet — HMS PINAFORE

Also during the fall of 1954, the Florida Symphony Youth Orchestra was officially organized, utilizing the young people who had received

34

free instruction and practice sessions from Symphony musicians during the previous season.

When the Women's Committee gathered that fall to begin their annual Symphony ticket sale campaign, there was excited discussion about the 'new' entertainment medium in town - television. Everyone had been glued to their TV to watch the World Series with its thousands of cheering spectators. Imagine the ladies' surprise when they were told that the Wall Street Journal had just reported that "Americans spend more money for Symphony concerts than for baseball game tickets..." It was their past experience that baseball tickets would be easier to sell, but the news heartened them for the big 'push'.

A few long-needed renovations were made in the old Municipal Auditorium that summer, in an effort to improve visibility and sound. It was a patch-up job, at best, but still an improvement. Nevertheless, complaints about the uncomfortable seats, drafts, and bad acoustics continued to be heard.

Including the Subscription Series in Orlando and Daytona Beach, the orchestra, during its fifth season, gave 39 concerts locally. In addition, single concerts were given in Mount Dora, Lake Wales and at Orlando Air Force Base. More than 30,000 school children heard the Symphony in 12 Youth Concerts in six Central Florida counties. Some of the symphony's musicians worked with the Bach Festival, a nationally-known annual event in Winter Park, and a string orchestra from the symphony presented a special program in Ocala. Local presentations included a ballet, the Symphony Ball, a POPS Concert, and a light opera, "The Gondoliers".

> The man that hath no music in himself,
> Nor is not moved with concord of sweet sounds,
> Is fit for treasons, stratagems, and spoils
> Let no such man be trusted.
> — Shakespeare

Local businessmen put their shoulders to the wheel. One of the more enlightened of these, the late William J. Capehart, then president of the First National Bank of Orlando, which provided sponsorship for Youth Concerts for Boone and Edgewater High Schools, stated: "The directors of the bank believe that industry and business have an obligation to the community, and should participate in its educational and cultural development."

The progress of, and improvement in the orchestra continued

steadily through the 1955-56 season - but the event most remembered about that season is that it ended without a deficit! In the black! That may be a crass remark to interject while remembering the uplifting atmosphere which pervaded the air when the Florida Symphony played. However, to the hard-working fund-raisers, always hearing that more and more money would be needed, it was the most beautiful music in the world. IN THE BLACK! Not only was it beautiful, it was a very unusual occurrence in the annals of symphony orchestras anywhere. Another impossible dream had come true for this amazing Florida Symphony!

Other things DID happen that year, however. David L. Cotton, former manager of the Savannah, Georgia, Symphony Orchestra, was hired as business manager to the Symphony, succeeding Robert Craig, who had accepted a civilian position with the U. S. Air Force.

> Dancing is the loftiest, the most moving,
> the most beautiful of the arts
> because it is no more translation
> or abstraction from life,
> it is life itself.
>
> — Havelock Ellis

A large audience enjoyed the beauty and technical excellence of the ballet program on January 14, 1956, when dancers from both Royal and Ebsen Schools of Dance presented "The Sleeping Beauty" and "La Boutique Fantastique". Having the professional Florida Symphony Orchestra play for them kept the graceful dancers on their toes.

The symphony continued its presentation of both Youth and Children's Concerts. Free musical instruction by members of the orchestra also continued, and ambitious youngsters began to look foward to careers in music, as they acquired the necessary proficiency.

The Florida Symphony Orchestra Singers, Frank Miller conducting, presented "Iolanthe", by Gilbert & Sullivan, in the early spring of 1956, under the sponsorship of the Altrusa Club of Orlando. A special Chamber Music program played by Symphony musicians Alphonse Carlo [violin], Rudolph Fischer ['cello], Thomas Benton [flute], Humphrey Van Dias [oboe], Emil Hebert [bassoon], and Katherine Carlo [piano], was presented on March 11, 1956 as a thank-you to symphony contributors in this season - the glorious season that ended in the black!

Of course, the Florida Symphony Society could never take a vacation. When one season ended in the spring, work had to start on

36

the coming season. Therefore, a general membership meeting was called for April 6, 1956, in the San Juan Hotel Ballroom. [Being a member was easy - dues were $5.00, or as much more as anyone wanted to donate.] At this meeting, plans were made to organize a new Arm of the Florida Symphony Society, to be called the "Associate Board". Members would be young adults, either single men and women or married couples. Once organized, they promptly adopted a project — sponsorship of the Ballet Concert for the 7th season.

Maestro Miller, in his quiet and undramatic way, had won great approval for his musical ability and conducting skill. The Millers, including sons David and Paul, had made warm friends in the area, and - without fanfare or flamboyance - Miller had maintained the high standards expected of him as the orchestra's conductor. His taste and excellent musical background had provided well-selected and varied programs which pleased the audiences.

Mr. and Mrs. Miller and Miss Helen Ryan, President of the FLorida Symphony Society, were guests of honor at the membership tea in late October, 1957, beginning the Symphony's eighth season. The tea was held at the home of Mr. & Mrs. Joseph D. Robinson, in Winter Park, and a large number of members and prospective members heard a delightful program of music by the Rollins Singers under the direction of Robert Hufstader.

The Florida Symphony ticket sale got off to a flying start in November, 1957, when a large crowd of workers gathered at the home of Mrs. Elwyn Evans for coffee, tickets and instructions. Then began a round of parties. So many benefit coffees, luncheons and teas were given, to arouse interest in the symphony, that even the newspaper took notice and came out with a bold, black headline: TEA AND SYMPHONY!

During this eighth season the Women's Committee, also, began holding membership luncheons, with guest artists as special guests. Luncheons were held the day preceding the concerts in which the artists were to appear, and gave members an opportunity to meet glamorous stars of the music world.

A series of Youth Concerts, by this time a well-established tradition with the orchestra, brought out ever-growing crowds of young people.

By this eighth season, the Subscription Series included eight concerts, the first of which was on January 2, 1958. Being right after the busy holiday season, it provided a welcome opportunity for a relaxed and serene surrender to the impeccably-played works of Tschaikovsky, Debussy, Dvorak and Wagner which had been chosen for the symphony's program. Soloists during this season included Earl Wild, Alphonse Carlo, Otto Silverstein, George London, Rudolf

Firkusny, Geraldine Gee, Jesse Pedrick Baker, and Eileen Farrell.

The eighth season's Gilbert & Sullivan light opera, on January 30, 1958, was the popular "Pirates of Penzance." It was directed with zest by Frank Miller, and the symphony musicians were also happy with the rollicking music.

A highlight of that 1957-58 season was the first Opera Gala, sponsored by the Junior League of Orlando for the benefit of the Florida Symphony. This was presented at the Municipal Auditorium in February, 1958, and drew music lovers from all over Florida. The Gala was in concert form, and featured famous opera stars Lisa Della Casa, Robert Merrill, Elena Nikolaidi, and Richard Tucker. It was a lustrous evening, handsomely staged and brilliantly performed - a full-dress affair.

An After-Gala breakfast at the Country Club of Orlando was sponsored by the League's Sustaining Members. A scene from "La Boheme" and the Quartet from "Rigoletto" were the featured Opera offerings.

The orchestra also presented concerts in surrounding Florida cities, as was their custom each season. The Chamber Music group, made up of musicians from the symphony, was much in demand by clubs, schools and other organizations. Edna Johnston was often the narrator for these programs.

There were more than a thousand symphony orchestras in the nation, but only forty of these were all-professional Metropolitan orchestras. The Florida Symphony Orchestra, now in its eighth season, was listed in the Top 40 of nationally-rated orchestras. Orlando was the only city in the United States with a population of under 100,000 which supported an orchestra.

One of the first events of the ninth season was an elegant fashion show, called a "Fol-de-rol", which was sponsored by the Orlando Downtown Council. This took place in April, after the close of the preceding season, and was an especially successful party from a financial standpoint.

Conductor Frank Miller gave a preview of the symphony programs planned for the ninth season, which would not only include the subscription series in Orlando and Daytona Beach, but concerts as usual in other Florida cities. One program would feature music of the three immortal B's - Bach, Beethoven, and Brahms. Contemporary music would be represented by the works of Morton Gould, Gardiner Rand, Aaron Copland, Turina, and Kadoly, and Ibert's "Suite Elizabethiane" would be given its first performance in the Southeastern United States at one memorable concert.

Maestro Miller trained a choir that fall, and his musicians played for the presentation of a beautiful program of Christmas choral music in Riverfront Park, Daytona Beach.

The orchestra also took part in the dedication of the new amphitheatre outdoors at Cypress Gardens, the world-famous beauty spot at Winter Haven, and their concert of Pops selections made a hit with the hundreds of tourists and townspeople visiting this popular Florida attraction.

It is always pleasant to learn of orchestra boosters from disparate backgrounds, and of the unusual ways in which the story of the orchestra is disseminated. During the ticket-selling campaign in the fall of 1958, Perfection Dairies printed a message on ten million milk cartons, which were distributed throughout Central Florida, urging all milk drinkers to be Florida Symphony concertgoers!

The Opera Gala concert sponsored by the Junior League of Orlando was given February 13, 1959, at the Municipal Auditorium. Metropolitan Opera stars Heidi Krall, Mildred Miller, Cesare Siepi, and Richard Tucker were the artists. Highlights of the evening were Gounod's Trio from "Faust", and the Quartet from Verdi's "Rigoletto." Siepi made a big hit with his rendition of "The Madamina" from Mozart's "Don Giovanni", this opera being one of Siepi's best showcases at the Metropolitan. One critic described him: "handsome, dashing, sly, gallant, brutal and irresistible . . . thrilling to hear a basso voice so fresh and adroit as his." The other singers also performed brilliantly in great operatic arias and duets, bringing the audience to a standing, shouting ovation time after time. It was an exciting evening. The Gala reception following was held at the home of Mr. and Mrs. R. D. Keene.

> There is music wherever there is
>   harmony, order, or proportion,
> and thus far we may maintain the music of the sphere.
>
> — Sir Thomas Brown

It was with much regret that the Florida Symphony Society Board received a letter of resignation from Conductor Frank Miller, to take effect at the end of the 1958-59 season. During his five-year tenure, Maestro Miller had brought the Florida Symphony a long way, and had earned praise from many sources. Mr. Miller was an internationally known 'Cellist, and while he had enjoyed his work as conductor, his first love was his instrument. When he was made an attractive offer to come as 'cellist with Fritz Reiner and the Chicago Symphony

Orchestra, he decided to take it. His letter of resignation denotes his innate sense of responsibility, and with what mixed feelings he had made his choice.

"It is with profound regret that I must notify you that I cannot accept further employment by the Florida Symphony after the termination of my present contract April 30, 1959."

"I have hastened to advise you at the earliest moment to afford you every opportunity to make your future plans."

"The past four years have been a period of great happiness and satisfaction for me and my family, and we look forward to making this season, my fifth as Conductor of the Florida Symphony Orchestra, the best year of all, musically."

"You have my assurance that I will do all in my power to complete the current season in an inspired manner and with the determination to reflect the highest artistic credit to the orchestra and to all of you who have given every support and encouragement to it."

A Resolution of Appreciation was sent to Mr. Miller for his services to the Florida Symphony Orchestra.

Maestro Frank Miller is remembered not only for his musicianship but for his unfailing courtesy with the orchestra. He was a well-organized conductor. One of his musicians said: "He always gave cues to bring in the players - we were never in doubt. He offered great confidence to everyone. His baton technique was excellent, carrying over the tradition of Toscanini."

Another friend commented: "For such a large man, his love for the miniature songs of Gilbert & Sullivan was, in a way, incongruous. He even wrote one of his own in their style. He was delighted to conduct Gilbert & Sullivan operettas and would sing every word as it went along, with the greatest amusement."

Perhaps the auciences remember best his fastidious, impeccable style of dressing, which was always in evidence. A musician remembers, "He gave infinite care to his full dress suits to see that they were not to be wrinkled in any way, or at any time." He set a good example not only for his musicians, but for his successor.

THE MAZER YEARS
A DYNAMIC PERIOD

Henry Mazer

As promised by Frank Miller, the concert season of 1958-59 had been an artistic and professional success, and concert-goers throughout Florida were sorry to bid Mr. Miller goodbye.

The new conductor, Henry Mazer, had been hired. He came to Orlando in March, 1959, to spend several days with Symphony Society directors planning the next season's programs. Mr. Mazer, who left a post as conductor of the Wheeling, West Virginia Symphony Orchestra which he had held for eleven years, was an intense, dynamic and ambitious 39-year-old man who had studied for the concert piano field before he began his career as orchestra conductor. He was gregarious, and met the public well. He was a good public speaker, and had an attractive family. Mazer was a protege of Fritz Reiner, and had been associated with Pierre Monteaux and the late Georges Enesco. He had also had been a guest conductor of the Chicago, Pittsburgh, Buffalo and National Symphony Orchestras.

The Florida Symphony tenth Anniversay season was coming up. In addition to the regular subscription series concerts, the orchestra had a number of other commitments. These included eight Youth Concerts [which played to more than 30,000 students in Orange County], several Sunday afternoon Pops Concerts, another spectacular Opera Gala [sponsored by the Junior League of Orlando], and a new series - the Lollipop Concerts - for very young children, under the auspices of the Associate Board.

Mount Dora organized the Mount Dora Symphony Society and encouraged the Mount Dora Kiwanis Club to sponsor their Florida Symphony concerts. Conductor Mazer met with the Society before the concerts for preview talks. It was good news to all concerned to learn that another community had formed its own Society to present concerts by the orchestra.

The operation of the Daytona Beach Symphony Society, which had been organized since the orchestra's second season, had been a strong support. Though at this time their subscription series still stood at five concerts, there was already talk about expanding to six.

The fall of 1959 was, as usual, a time for fund-raising and ticket-selling. New members were sought by all Arms of the Symphony. Members of the Associate Board were excited about the

42

new 'Lollip Concerts' for youngsters of first, second and third grade level, introducing beginners to fine music. Henry Mazer was just the person to encourage this activity, as he had young people in his own household.

> The grand object of music is to touch the heart.
>
> — Karl Bach

In December, 1959, some seventy wide-eyed young concertgoers sat in a circle on the floor of the San Juan Hotel ballroom and heard the very first Florida Symphony Lollipop Concert. It was quite a sight to see! After playing good music to this engaging group, and explaining as it progressed, Maestro Mazer distributed real lollipops to the children as a reward for their polite attention. They were close enough to the musicians to satisfy their curiosity, and it was a time of wonder for them - and for their parents!

The symphony's tenth season opened on January 7, 1960. For his 'debut', Henry Mazer had selected a program that was appropriately brilliant and challenging, giving a foretaste of what the season promised. An informal after-concert party at the Amherst Apartments, sponsored by the Women's Committee, provided a great variety of food and drink. It also provided concertgoers an opportunity to meet the musicians - who were relaxing after a taxing performance - and congratulate them on a great concert.

The Opera Gala for this season - by now an established annual event - featured highlights from "La Traviata", with Metropolitan Opera stars Dorothy Kirsten, Theodor Uppman, and Cesare Vallette - in costume - exhibiting their acting as well as their singing talents in the beautifully-staged scenes. The After-Opera reception was held at the home of Mr. and Mrs. Charles O Andrews, in Winter Park, and was sponsored again by the Sustaining members of the Junior League.

The 1960 Symphony Champagne Ball, sponsored by the Associate Board, was held on St. Patrick's Day evening, at the Country Club of Orlando. The full orchestra played for the first part of the evening, and a combo comprised of Florida Symphony members played for dancing afterward.

Altogether, that tenth season was a successful one, liberally sprinkled with specials and extras, chamber music concerts, out-of-town tours, Youth Concerts, and a plethora of music-related events.

And even before the next season began, something new was undertaken.

The Florida Symphony Society held a Piano Competition for young pianists of Central Florida. Mrs. Walter B. Johnston was chairman for this pilot enterprise, and competition was keen. Roland Penny, 15, was the winner over fourteen other entrants, and was later featured as soloist with the full symphony at one of the 1961 Youth Concerts.

David Cotton, who had been business manager of the symphony for three years, resigned in April, 1960, to assume the position of sales promotion manager for Howard Johnson Company, in Miami. Cotton had been a popular young bachelor in Orlando, and promised to return as frequently as possible to hear the symphony and to visit friends.

The largest fashion show to date was presented by the Women's Committee on September 15, 1960, in the Egyptian Room of the Cherry Plaza Hotel. Sponsored by the Downtown Merchants Association, the show featured fashions for men, women, and children, and was highly successful from both an entertainment and a monetary standpoint.

The annual ballet program on December 27, 1960, was a joyous delayed Christmas gift to all of Central Florida. Central Florida's own Barbara Fleming and Kip Watson, on leave from New York engagements, plus Linda Yourth and Paul Nickel of the Andre Eglevsky company and New York City Ballet, led dancers from Central Florida ballet schools in the enchanting "Cinderella". Edith Royal choreographed the production, adhering closely to traditional lines, and music — of course — was provided by the Florida Symphony. "Cinderella" was so much in demand that it was repeated both in Daytona Beach and Mount Dora.

The 11th season's Opera Gala, sponsored still by the Junior League of Orlando, was especially memorable. Metropolitan Opera stars Eleanor Steber, Jan Peerce, and Cornell MacNeil contributed both dramatic power and vocal pyrotechnics to their presentation of Acts I and II of "Tosca", as well as Marochallin's Monologue from "Der Rosenkavalier", arias from "Otello" and the trio from "Il Trovatore."

It was a busy 15-week season. A group from the symphony formed a Chamber Music Orchestra which appeared at various clubs and concerts, while the full orchestra presented its accustomed schedule of subscription series concerts, out-of-town concerts, youth and Lollipop concerts, ballet, Opera Gala, and so on. One of the most-talked about concerts of the season occurred on February 16, 1961, when Maestro Mazer programmed the resplendent "Pines of Rome" by Ottorino Respighi. Twenty-nine additional brass players were strategically placed in the balcony and at the back of the auditorium,

44

and when the music reached its climax, it was a shattering one, indeed! Suddenly, from both the stage, the balcony, and the back of the house came a great burst of sound, as the brasses brought the work to a dramatic, fortissimo conclusion. The audience stood wildly applauding for long minutes after the concert was over.

Another unusual treat of the 1961 season was the Women's Committee-sponsored POPS Concert featuring John Sebastian, the harmonica whiz. Mr. Sebastian had appeared with the Philadelphia Orchestra under Ormandy, as well as the New York Philharmonic, Cleveland Orchestra, Boston Symphony, Chicago Symphony, and Tokyo Symphony. The audience was both amazed and delighted at what this unique artist could do with such a lowly instrument as the harmonica.

During its 11th season, the Symphony commissioned a young American composer, Eddy Manson - already well-known in the popular music field - to write a symphony. Manson came to Orlando to conduct the full orchestra in the premiere performance of his Symphony Number One. It was in the traditional four movements, but purely American in feeling, making use of modern musical language and sounds and reflecting a jazz influence. It was well-received by the audience, and received good reviews.

The main dining room of the Country Club of Orlando was transformed into a Japanese garden, with bamboo, hanging baskets, trailing flowers, and a real waterfall, when the Symphony Ball was held on March 17, 1961.

The Florida Symphony had made such a hit with Florida's Governor, Farris Bryant, and Mrs. Bryant, when they came to Orlando to attend the Opera Gala, that the Governor invited the symphony to come to Tallahassee to present a concert at Florida State University. It was held on the opening day of the State Legislature, April 4, 1961, and though our legislators may have had moments of discord later in that session, at least opening day was completely 'harmonious'.

The early '60's were the 'heyday' of Florida Symphony POPS presentations, because there was little else in the area featuring big-name popular artists. The final POPS of the 1961 season was a smash hit, called "An Evening on Broadway", starring recording, musical comedy, and TV favorites Lois Hunt and Earl Wrightson. They sang top hits from Broadway shows for a light-hearted program to end the season.

> You call it a waste of time; This taste For popular Tunes,
>   and yet Goodbye to care when you whistle the air
> Of the song that you can't forget.
> — Guy Wetmore Carryl

Van Cliburn with Helen Ryan, Symphony
Society President,
in January, 1962

And this light-hearted mood continued as the Symphony Society began making plans for the following season. Chief reason for the gaiety - and even excitement - was that they had managed to book the sensational young pianist, Van Cliburn, for the January 24, 1962 concert. Riding largely on the strength of Cliburn's fame and enormous popularity, the Florida Symphony's twelfth season was - for the first time - a complete sellout! The growing excellence of the orchestra, itself, naturally had some bearing on this happy turn of events; but however many the contributing factors, the end result was a dream come true for symphony supporters.

The Florida Symphony Society announced a new competition - this time to be statewide - for pianists, violinists and 'cellists not over 19 years of age. Regional competitions were held in February in Tallahassee, Jacksonville, Gainesville, Orlando, Tampa and Miami. Those who made it through both regional and semi-final competitions came to Orlando for the finals. Expenses of all finalists and semi-finalists were paid, from their home to point of competition, by the Symphony Society. Final winners were John Frusciante, Ft. Lauderdale; Mimi Johnson, Gainesville; and George Atwell, Orlando.

The Women's Committee, in cooperation with the Downtown Orlando Council, Inc., again sponsored a fashion show in September, 1961, in the Egyptian Room of the Cherry Plaza Hotel. A capacity crowd of more than one thousand people not only ogled the fashions, but heard Henry Mazer speak on the need for a new Concert Hall with proper acoustics, stage, and seating. The theme of the fashion show was a popular one - "Courtship to Music" - but the theme of Mr. Mazer's speech proved much MORE popular, as it is still being heard today.

The Children's Concerts [an expansion on the original 'Lollipop' Series sponsored by the Associate Board] were special productions in 1961-62. "Alice in Wonderland", in December of 1961, featured authentically-costumed dancers of the Ballet Royal, depicting Alice, the White Rabbit, the Mad Hatter, the Queen of Hearts, et al, to the delight of both children and parents. Ravel's short opera, "The Bewitched Child", was staged in February, 1962. Maestro Mazer had auditioned dozens of singers to form a company for this presentation. Their months of rehearsal were repaid in full by the enthusiastic audience reception given their efforts.

Another special event of the season occurred on December 16, 1961, when Henry Mazer and members of the Florida Symphony joined with choirs from ten Orlando and Winter Park churches to present a beautiful program titled "Songs of Christmas". Proceeds from the program benefitted the Central Florida Museum.

In 1961-62, the orchestra played more than fifty concerts during its 15-week season, leaving the musicians somewhat breathless after it was all over. Included in their appearances had been a CBS-TV national network program, "Look Up and Live", on which the orchestra had been featured together with the Bach Festival and Rollins Chapel Choirs. On this occasion, Martin Gabel, well-known actor, was narrator for the "King David Oratorio." The live audience was amazed at the amount of equipment that was brought in for the telecast.

1962's Opera Gala surpassed all its glamorous predecessors. This was the Junior League of Orlando's fifth annual production, and they brought to it their years of experience as well as months of planning and hard work. Selections from Verdi's "Rigoletto" and Strauss' "Die Fledermaus" were gloriously sung by opera stars Walter Cassel, Mildred Miller, Brian Sullivan, and Roberta Peters. A torrential rain didn't discourage opera lovers at all; the auditorium was filled by show time. Afterward, some 400 guests attended the breakfast for the stars at the Country Club of Orlando.

By this time, it was no longer a surprise when nationally-known music critics 'dropped in', unheralded, for a concert. Harold C. Schonbert, of the New York Times, and Dr. Paul Henry Lang, of the New York Herald Tribune, were two who so favored the orchestra in 1962.

Also 'new in '62' were the dinner-and-music parties sponsored at the elegant 'Maison et Jardin' restaurant by owner-hosts Mr. and Mrs. Harold R. Walsh. The Walshes were true patrons of the arts, and planned several 'musical dinners' at their suburban dining place. Invited guests were served gourmet food, then entertained by members of the Florida Symphony playing after-dinner concerts.

An annual "special event" was the Symphony Ball, a glittering affair, held again on St. Patrick's Day at the Country Club of Orlando.

In the fall of 1962, as the orchestra began its 13th season, nobody - apparently - considered '13' in any way unlucky. Indeed, the Florida Symphony had the largest advance sale of season tickets in its history, even without the 'sales help' of the previous season's star attraction, Van Cliburn.

The by-now-familiar round of concerts of all types continued unabated. The number of Youth Concerts was increased, both in Orange County and throughout the State. The orchestra again joined various church groups in presenting "Songs of Christmas", and St. Patrick's Day marked another glamorous Symphony Ball.

The Children's Series [sponsored by the Associate Board] was again a noteworthy achievement. On December 22, the familiar children's

48

opera, "Amahl and the Night Visitors" was presented, and on January 5 they 'hauled out the big guns' by bringing Captain Kangaroo, every child's favorite TV personality, for a live-and-in-person production titled "Fun With Music". The children were ecstatic! The final program on this memorable series was the beautiful "Hansel and Gretel" ballet on February 2, again teaming the Florida Symphony and the dancers of the Ballet Royal.

The very first completely-staged opera attmepted in Orlando took place on February 8, 1963, when the Junior League of Orlando brought Richard Tucker, Teresa Stratas, Heidi Krall and Mac Morgan - straight from the Metropolitan Opera - to headline their production of "La Boheme". Some of the stars were making return engagements, so they were greeted as old friends. It was a smashing success in every way - and a far cry from the first Opera Gala in concert form held only six years previously.

After the close of the 1962-63 season, and as one of the end-of-school festivities, the Florida Symphony presented the "Philharmonic Follies" for the benefit of Orange County high school students. The Follies were held at the San Juan Hotel ballroom, and students danced to a 'Best of Broadway' variety of hit music. This event was sponsored by the Hi-Y and Tri-Hi-Y clubs of the various high schools, and was greatly enjoyed by the young crowd.

At the annual meeting of the Symphony Society in the spring of 1963, George W. Johnson was named as the new President, succeeding Miss Helen Ryan, who had held the post for seven years. Miss Ryan, in turn, was elected to the new post of Executive Vice President, becoming a paid employee of the orchestra after thirteen years of invaluable and uninterrupted volunteer service.

The fourteenth season of the Florida Symphony was heralded by the Women's Committee's October luncheon for old and new members. The three young musicians who had won the Symphony's competition during the previous season were featured on the program. This public appearance served as an excellent springboard for the announcement of the Symphony Society's third annual state competition, once more for students of piano, violin and 'cello.

The orchestra benefited from a colorful event, the 'Bar Harbor Banquet', a real New England shore dinner, sponsored in November by the Winter Park Junior Service League. It was held at the Seminole Hotel, and Ron Galli's orchestra provided continuous entertainment, with strolling musicians assisting.

And so the 14th season of the Florida Symphony Orchestra was launched, with great enthusiasm. The word spread rapidly that there would be a return engagement of the tremendously popular pianist,

Van Cliburn, who had created such a sensation on his first appearance in Orlando. To add to that, the world-famous Isaac Stern, also making his second appearance, had been booked, plus Cesare Seipi, the handsome basso from the Met — and those were only headliners on the list of artists booked for the season. To accomodate the many scheduled concerts and other musical events, the symphony season was, this year, increased to sixteen weeks.

The 14th season's annual Women's Committee Fall Fashion Show was held, this year, at the Municipal Auditorium, on September 19. The extra seating space was needed to accomodate the crowds who came to see Bess Myerson, star of radio and TV and a former 'Miss America', who was fashion commentator. The show was called "I Dreamed I Went Around the World", with fashions provided by the Downtown Orlando Council, Inc., and modeled by a bevy of excited local models.

The Women's Committee also sponsored a bridge-party-series for the benefit of the symphony that season, adding still another fund-raising project to the many undertaken through the years. The bridge parties were held in a private dining room at the Cherry Plaza Hotel, and were very well-attended.

> Any man's death diminishes me,
>   because I am involved in mankinde . . .
>
> — John Donne

Conductor Henry Mazer, now in his fifth year as Maestro, decided to begin the 1963-64 season's opening concert with Beethoven's titanic third Symphony, the "Eroica", . . . to be played in memory of the nation's so-recently slain President, John Fitzgerald Kennedy, who had done more to encourage the arts and bring recognition to artists than any of his predecessors. The composer himself had written of the "Eroica" that it was "in memory of a great man." In its passages of profound sorrow and indomitable courage, it seemed a fitting tribute to President Kennedy.

The Associate Board's Children's Series this season included - in December - the very first Orlando production of Tchaikovsky's full-length ballet, "The Nutcracker", staged by the Ballet Royal. So ambitious was this undertaking - and so magnificent were the sets, costumes, choreography and music - that an evening performance of the ballet was held for the enjoyment of symphony subscribers, following the afternoon performance for children. Rounding out an exceptionally successful season, the Associate Board presented the animated musical fantasy, "Babar, the Elephant", in January [and repeated the program in Daytona Beach], and in February, the beloved Captain Kangaroo, in person, returned with a second "Fun With Music" crowd-pleaser.

The Women's Committee, not to be outdone, featured "An Evening With Jose Melis" as the January POPS Concert, followed by "Broadway Songbook" in February, and "Gaite Parisienne - Music in the French Manner" in March.

The Junior League of Orlando presented their second fully-staged opera - Bizet's "Carmen" - in 1964, and brought Metropolitan Opera stars Jean Madeira, Annaliese Rothenberger, Guiseppe Campore and Norman Treigle to headline the dazzling performance.

Jean Madeira, Annaliese Rothenberger, Guiseppe Campore and Norman Treigle rehearse "Carmen" with Maestro Henry Mazer.

The Daytona Beach Symphony Society added a sixth concert to their Subscription Series, and out-of-town concerts for the orchestra multiplied. Youth Concerts were played for more than 50,000 school children throughout the state.

In the fund-raising department, the Junior Service League of Winter Park's annual benefit took the form of a colorful Texas Bar-B-Q, where folk singers wandered and costumed guests had a great time learning to square-dance. The annual Symphony Ball on March 14 was again held at the Country Club of Orlando, and as always brought social leaders and music lovers together for an evening of music, pleasure, and dancing.

Once again a distinguished array of guest stars was signed for the orchestra's 15th season. These included the tremendously popular Eileen Farrell, soprano, and - since Henry Mazer was always full of surprises - another 'first' for the Subscription Series. This was the appearance of dancer-narrator Felicia Montealegri [Mrs. Leonard Bernstein] and Broadway actor Michael Wager - quite a radical departure from the traditional pianist - violinist - vocalist guest artists — and both were extremely well-received in their narration of Honegger's "Jeanne d'Arc au Bucher."

On May 10, 1964, the Florida Symphony Training Orchestra[also called Youth Orchestra] under the direction of Joseph Kreines, assistant conductor of the Florida Symphony, presented their first public concert of the season in the Annie Russell Theater at Rollins College, Winter Park. These 58 young musicians, junior and senior high school students, received instruction without charge from the professional musicians of the Florida Symphony. Their future goals included establishment of a string program in one or more junior high schools, and funding scholarships for talented students who would not otherwise be able to afford further musical education.

Eva Gabor, actress, of the beautiful Hungarian Gabor sisters, was fashion commentator for the annual Women's Committee Fashion Show, held on September 17, 1964. Eva also appeared in an amusing skit, "If I Were President", written especially for this show by Ruth Robinson, of Orlando, pianist and writer. The show was held at the Municipal Auditorium, with fashions again furnished by the Downtown Orlando Council, Inc.

This season was not without sadness, however. Miss Joy Hawley, who had been a staunch friend of the orchestra since its inception, passed away on August 31, 1964. Her many contributions are noted in her story in the chapter on "Angels". Suffice it to say that her friends were legion, and though they felt her loss keenly, they worked even harder to nurture the symphony she had loved so well.

52

At the annual Women's Committee luncheon at the Country Club of Orlando in October, it was announced that the Committee, in cooperation with the Theater Arts Department of Rollins College, would present "The Three Penny Opera" during the Christmas holidays. Some excerpts from that production were part of the luncheon program. Bernard Bailie sang "Mack the Knife", other performers sang less-familiar songs from the opera, and Arthur Wagner, director of Rollins' Theater Arts Department, gave a synopsis of the plot. There have been lots of luncheons over the years, but this is an exceptionally well-remembered one.

The Associate Board's Children's Series was still riding a crest of popularity, and no wonder. They opened the season on December 28 with the lively and colorful "Coppelia", in conjunction with the Ballet Royal. Subsequent programs were "Peter and the Wolf" and "Carnival of the Animals", narrated by the incomparable Basil Rathbone, and the children's opera, "Jack and the Beanstalk".

Oh music, sphere-descended maid
Friend of pleasure, wisdom's aid!
— *William Collins*

The Women's Committee, in conjunction with the Rollins Conservatory of Music, presented "The Art of Listening", a series of eight lectures on music, given by Mrs. Arnold J. Wilson, Jr. The popular lectures paralleled the eight Subscription Series concerts, and were held at Martin Hall, off the Rollins College Campus.

POPS Concerts that season featured Skitch Henderson in January, Peter Nero and his piano styling in March, and a "Broadway Songbook" program [also in January] that starred local artists - whose reception was every bit as enthusiastic as that given the nationally-famous stars.

The Symphony season was again extended, from 16 weeks to 17. Another week, another payroll. Fund-raising activities continued apace. The Winter Park Junior Service League's now-annual benefit was called a "Gas Light Gala". Handlebar mustaches and Gay Nineties costumes were in evidence. The food was bountiful, the music was happily rinky-dink. It was fun to fund the Florida Symphony!

A 'Symphonic Boutique Bazaar' was held in December at the Prado of Proctor Center, Winter Park, for the benefit of the orchestra. It was organized by a group of Women's Committee members who liked to make hand-made gifts. Mrs. Leslie Sawyer and Mrs. Clifford Rees were co-chairmen, and their unique gift collection brought shoppers from all over the area.

The Symphony Ball was held at the Country Club of Orlando, which had been decorated with Spanish galleons shimmering with jewels and golden pirate treasures. After the champagne buffet, the Florida Symphony played waltzes for the first hour, and Jerry Lyons and his orchestra played for dancing the remainder of the evening.

The Opera Gala, still under the auspices of the Junior League of Orlando, presented the fully-staged production of "La Traviata" on February 12. Guest artists were Met stars Phyllis Curtin, Franco Ghitti, and Mario Sereni, with a large number of local choristers in supporting roles.

Any event, any media, that benefits the Florida Symphony Orchestra is always welcome, since money is the only thing the symphony always lacks. Therefore, the Associate Board jumped at the chance to sponsor the April 14, 1965 premiere of the Rogers & Hammerstein motion picture, "The Sound of Music", when it was shown at the Beacham Theater in downtown Orlando. Members of the orchestra presented a concert at 7:30 P.M. prior to the eight o'clock showing of the picture. Downtown Orlando Council, Inc., arranged for free parking in the new parking facility west of the theater, for show guests. The Robert Meyer Motor Inn put on a special "Sound of Music" dinner from 6 to 8 p.m., featuring Austrian dishes appropriate to the movie's theme. It was a successful benefit, and everyone was pleased with the picture and the lavish door prizes.

Prior to the opening of its sixteenth season, the orchestra was well-represented at the National Conference of the American Symphony Orchestra League in Washington, D.C., June 16-17, 1965, by Robert T. Anderson, Symphony Society president, and Mrs. Anderson; Miss Helen Ryan, executive vice-president of the Society and past Conference chairman; Mrs. Luther K. Jennings, president of the Women's Committee; and Mrs. Arnold J. Wilson, Jr., Society vice-president, who was also Regional Chairman of the Women's Council of the League and Chairman of the Awards Committee.

The Andersons attended a pre-conference White House Festival of the Arts at which Mrs. Lyndon Johnson, then first lady, was hostess. Many distinguished speakers were heard at the Conference, placing emphasis on the promotion of the arts in the United States.

Combined church choirs and the Florida Symphony Orchestra opened the sixteenth season with the presentation of a special program on December 16, 1965 - Handel's always beloved "Messiah". Featured soloists were Doris Yorick, Dorothy Hepburn, John McCol-

Mr. & Mrs. Luther K. Jennings, Mrs. Arnold J Wilson, Miss Helen Ryan, and Mrs. Robert T. Anderson pictured at the American Symphony Orchestra League National Conference in the nation's capitol during June, 1965.

lum, and William Warfield. The soloists read their parts from hand-held vocal scores [it IS a long oratorio] with the exception of Mr. Warfield, who knew every word and note from memory, and whose magnificent basso voice rang with the emotion of the music.

> *He could fiddle all the bugs*
> *Off a sweet potato vine.*
>
> *— Stephen Vincent Benet*

A new concertmaster and assistant conductor, Carter Nice, of New York, joined the orchestra this season. His name was familiar, as he was the grandson of the late Carter Nice, a former director of the Rollins Conservatory of Music. Mr. Nice succeeded Chilean violinist, Patricio Salvatierra, who had returned to his homeland.

The three-concert POPS Series was especially noteworthy this season. The late, great Duke Ellington was a strong drawing-card for the opening concert. The second featured "Music of the Roaring Twenties" with Patricia Puckett, a former 'Miss Mississippi' as guest entertainer. The final POPS of the season was an all-Gershwin program, featuring the Florida Symphony and Joela Jones, brilliant young pianist, guest soloist.

This, too, was the season that the ineffable Jack Benny came to Orlando to play a benefit with the orchestra. The date was January 28, 1966. So great was Benny's appeal that even Governor Hayden Burns and Mrs. Burns flew down from Tallahassee to enjoy the show. Benny raised some six million dollars for symphony orchestras in the United States during his lifetime, and brought his violin playing [not as bad as he pretended] and droll comments to symphony audiences over many years. He was a real music lover, and when he was helping good music to survive, he was happiest. It was a great loss to music, as well as to his millions of friends, when Mr. Benny died in late December, 1974.

The Florida Symphony made its first 'international appearance' when it went to the Bahamas in January, 1966, to perform at Tupperware's annual Distributor's Conference, being held at the Jack Tar Hotel on Grand Bahama Island. The performance was a surprise for the Tupperware distributors who had come from all over the United States and a number of foreign countries. The shipboard crossing, though short, was a rough one, and a sizeable portion of the orchestra got so seasick they never expected to live or play music ever again. Notwithstanding, everyone recovered upon arrival at Grand Bahama, and their presentation was nothing short of triumphant.

music is my rampart, and my only one.
— John Stuart Mill

1966 was also a good year for dance. The Children's Series opened with the ballet, "The Sad Princess", choreographed by Carolyn Bourland, of Carolyn's School of Dance. The second program starred world-famous ballerina, Maria Tallchief, with the Ballet Royal, in "Les Sylphides", and the Ballet Royal dancers completed the program with Act II of "The Nutcracker". "Les Sylphides" is technically very demanding for the corps de ballet, but Edith Royal's young dancers acquitted themselves to perfection. Maria Tallchief herself said so!

In March, the orchestra played for the Gala Performance of the Southeastern Regional Ballet Festival. Ballet companies from all the Southeastern states were in attendance, and eight specifically-chosen ballets were presented on the Gala. It was an exceptional treat for these lovely and talented young dancers to be supported by a full symphony orchestra, and their performance was a true delight.

56

Birgit Nilsson, one of the great Wagnerian sopranos of the age, was the Stellar attraction at the final concert of the 1965-66 Subscription Series. It was a memorable experience. Her interpretation of the passionate Love-Death [Liebestod] music from Wagner's "Tristan and Isolde" and the visionary "Elsa's Dream" from "Lohengrin" displayed the extraordinary power and contrasting softness of her great voice.

"Madame Butterfly" was the presentation of the Junior League of Orlando's Opera Gala this season. Stars of the beautifully staged and costumed production were Lucine Amara, Helen Vanni, John Alexander and Frank Guerrera. In April, 1966, shortly after the presentation of "Butterfly", the Junior League - sponsors of the Opera Gala productions since their inception - decided that the time had come for the organization of an Opera Gala Guild. Mrs. Benjamin Abberger, Jr., chairman of the Florida Symphony Society's Steering Committee, and Mrs. Robert Neel, Chairman of the Junior League Steering Committee, sent letters to a number of music lovers in the area, inviting them to become members of the Opera Gala Guild. Transition of Opera sponsorship from the Junior League to the new Guild was to take place over a three-year period to assure continuity, and to provide the Junior League's experience to the Guild.

The Florida Symphony, through the years, has been nothing if not versatile. In January, 1966, when the Mount Dora music group planned a program "A Touch of Vienna," for their POPS Concert, the orchestra played selections from Strauss, Brahms and Lehar. Jack Thompson and Gail Divine were featured as soloists, and were joined by two other vocalists in selections from "The Merry Widow". Though the music transported the delighted audience to the banks of the Blue Danube and the shaded walkways of the Viennese Woods, the program was actually held at the Mount Dora Community Building, and was sponsored by the Mount Dora Kiwanis Club as a benefit for the symphony.

The Children's Concerts that year were more versatile than ever, presenting a fast-moving program featuring the Mar-Chris Marionettes; a lesson on "How to Conduct A Symphony Orchestra", narrated by local radio and TV personality, Walt Sickles; and the ever-popular ballet program, with the talented young members of the Ballet Royal.

Everything was in high gear, and going magnificently. But an interruption was in the wings.

Before season's end, Henry Mazer, conductor of the orchestra since 1957, tendered his resignation, to be effective April 30, 1966.

Robert T. Anderson, President of the Florida Symphony Society, wrote these words in accepting Mr. Mazer's resignation:

"I sincerely regret Mr. Mazer's terminating his highly-satisfactory service with the Florida Symphony Society, and wish him continued success in the years to come. The Symphony Board recognizes the unique contribution which Henry Mazer has made to the musical and cultural life of our community."

"He is a musician of exceptional ability. He has served as Conductor of the Florida Symphony Orchestra during a period of great growth and enormous activity."

Despite Mazer's resignation, the activity continued. The Symphony Ball's theme for the 16th season was "Camelot" - rather appropriate, under the circumstances - and the Country Club of Orlando was transformed into a truly royal King Arthur's Court. The Ball was a proper grace note on which to conclude another successful season.

A PERIOD OF TRANSITION —
THE YEAR OF GUEST CONDUCTORS

Yuri Krasnopolsky
[Resident Conductor]

Minas Christian

George Trautwein

Joseph Levine

Hermann Herz

The 'Mazer era' was over. Until a permanent new musical director could be selected, the Board decided that a series of well-known guest conductors would be invited to direct during this seventeenth season of the Florida Symphony Orchestra. Yuri Krasnopolsky, formerly an assistant conductor of the New York Philharmonic, was named 'resident' conductor for the season. Guest conductors were Minas Christian, George Trautwein, Joseph Levine, and Hermann Herz.

More than five hundred women members of the Women's Committee rang doorbells in the spring, canvassing Orlando, Winter Park and Maitland in an all-out effort to make the Florida Symphony a 'household word', and something of personal value and interest to all the people in the area. Using the slogan "A Dollar Today, A Symphony Tomorrow", they worked diligently to expand the base of support for the orchestra by recruiting more small contributors - and more large contributors, too, when possible.

They must have had a premonition of coming events, for the big news came in July, 1966. After months of hard work by Robert Anderson, Helen Ryan, and others on the Board, the announcement was made that the Florida Symphony was one of sixty-one orchestras in thirty-three states chosen to share in $80.2 million in grants from the Ford Foundation. The news rated banner headlines in the Sentinel-Star, and symphony supporters were jubilant.

The Ford grant to the Florida Symphony consisted of expendable funds in the amount of $100,000, payable at $20,000 per year over the next five years, for the express purpose of strengthening the existing orchestra; and $500,000 in an Endowment Fund. Conditions of the Grant stipulated that, over the next five years, the community must match this amount with $500,000 raised locally, and put specifically in an unencumbered Matching Fund. The complete story of the Ford Foundation grant appears elsewhere in this book, but no words can adequately describe the exhiliration generated by this breath-taking news when it was first made public.

One of the first major benefits specifically intended to swell the Ford matching fund was given on February 3, 1967, when the popular pianist, Van Cliburn, returned to Orlando for a special concert. Minute Maid and Tupperware each underwrote one-third of his fee, so that virtually all the proceeds of the event could go directly into the Ford Fund.

And the night shall be filled with music
And the cares that infest the day,
Shall fold their tents, like the Arabs,
And as silently steal away.

— Longfellow

The orchestra continued its dizzying pace, presenting a total of over sixty-five programs during the season. The Opera Gala Guild, on its own for the first time, presented "The Barber of Seville", as successfully as if the Guild had been doing such things for years. Yuri Krasnopolsky conducted all three Children's Concerts, which included the ballet "Hansel and Gretel", staged by the Ballet Royal; Reginald DeKoven's "Robin Hood", a program based on the classic hero dear to the hearts of the young audience; and the "Introduction to Musical Appreciation", actually an educational program, but it especially intrigued the children since it was titled "Baton Man", with the 'melody drama' unabashedly modeled after the popular 'Batman' TV show.

The first POPS was a "Fiesta Musicale" featuring Jose melis, brought back by popular demand. George Trautwein, associate conductor of the Minneapolis Symphony, conducted the program. The second POPS, with the theme, "Ports of Call", presented a potpourri of international musical favorites, and featured the Florida Symphony under the direction of Yuri Krasnopolsky. The final POPS Concert brought the popular stage, screen, and TV singer, Johnny Desmond, featured in an appropriately-titled "Oh, Johnny" program, with Hermann Herz, music director of the Duluth Symphony, on the podium.

The orchestra took part in a series of outdoor entertainments planned for the Mead Garden Amphitheatre, giving a concert there in March, 1967. The audience enjoyed the beautiful music in this lovely and unusual setting. The program, a varied one with many popular favorites, was sponsored by the Cultural Events Committee of the Winter Park Chamber of Commerce.

"Paris in the Spring" was the theme for the Symphony Ball at the Country Club of Orlando in April of 1967. The Club was filled with green and blue paper flowers, festive and very much in decorative style that season. The Florida Symphony, conducted by Dr. Ward Woodbury, of Rollins College, played tunes like "Springtime in Paris" and other Broadway-type selections with a 'foreign flair', which made a great hit with the audience.

So, without missing a beat, the Florida Symphony sailed through this 'year of guest conductors'. The musicians had shown their ability to adjust to the leadership of conductors with different styles and interpretations in this Year of Transition, but were looking forward to 'settling in' with a permanent conductor. After much soul searching, the Board announced its choice.

THE PRUSSIAN PERIOD — The Herz Years

He had never heard such music as this,
never dreamt such music was possible.
He was conscious, while it lasted, that he
saw deeper into the beauty, the sadness
of things, the very heart of them, and
their pathetic evanescence, as with a new
inner eye — even into eternity itself,
beyond the veil.

"Trilby" — George Louis Palmella
[Busson du Maurier]

Hermann Herz

Hermann Herz had excellent credentials. He was reputed to be a perfectionist. He was a man who liked music of many types, and he explained the balance he was continually striving for in his programs: "It encompasses the old and the new idioms as well as the familiar and unfamiliar in both fields. I also try to cover a wide range of nationalities and periods in music."

Hermann Herz was born and educated in Germany. A graduate of the State Academy of Music in Munich, he was active in the Munich Opera, the Berlin Opera, and at the St. Gallen [Switzerland] Municipal Theatre. When in Duluth, he introduced Grand Opera in that city.

Before World War II, he emigrated to Johannesburg, South Africa, where he conducted opera, ballet, symphony and radio-symphony concerts locally and internationally. Members of his family are still living in Johannesburg, and he and Mrs. Herz and many of their friends often go there for visits.

Serge Koussevitzky brought Herz to the United States in 1948 to head the Opera Department of the Berkshire Music Festival, in Tanglewood. Musical directorship for Television Opera in New York and Mercury Recording assignments followed.

Subsequent summer experiences as director of concerts in St. Paul, Minneapolis, and New Orleans led to his positions as guest conductor of the Chicago Grant Park Orchestra, the Minneapolis and Connecticut Symphonies, and the Philharmonic Orchestras of Tulsa, Oklahoma, and Toronto, Canada.

Herz had been guest conductor and lecturer at the Universities of Indiana, Wisconsin, Iowa and Minneapolis, and had also served in many educational, cultural and entertainment media. He came to Orlando in May, 1967, to have preliminary discussions with Board members of the Symphony Society so that he could begin planning his programs for the upcoming season.

In August of 1967, Herz also auditioned vocal soloists for various orchestra performances during the 1967-68 season, and sub-principals for the Opera Gala production, "Faust".

The resultant 'Florida Symphony Opera Gala Guild Chorus' presented several concerts during the late summer and fall of that year, in Hooker Hall, a part of First Congregational Church, Winter Park. Proceeds from these programs enabled fourteen high school students and their advisors to attend a three-week work camp in Puerto Rico.

When not giving concerts, the Chorus was already busily rehearsing for the February Opera production.

The orchestra extended its season from eighteen to twenty weeks, and expanded the number of musicians to 75. A total of 75 concerts was scheduled for the season, and activities continued apace. In addition, the Florida Youth Symphony, a successor to the former Youth Training Orchestra, was activated by Conductor Hermann Herz.

In September, the Winter Park Junior Service League's annual dinner dance, for the benefit of the symphony, was held at Rio Pinar Country Club. With the theme, "Hurricane Happening", all weather signs pointed to a fun-filled evening. The 'Top Hats' from Valdosta, Georgia, played for dancing.

The Women's Committee held their annual fund-raising Fashion Show on October 28. It was staged at the Orange Blossom Playhouse, and was called 'Coronet Rose.' Miss Todd Ryan, of New York, was the commentator, and real beauty queens - Jane Ann Jayroe, 1967 Miss America; Cheri Bauer, Miss Orlando '67; Chira Kirkland, Miss Winter Park '67; Donna Crenshaw, Miss Missouri, '53; Alice Bennett, Miss Missouri, '55; Pat Mulcahy, Miss Hawaii, '66; Sue Foreman, Miss St. Petersburg, '59; Lynda Harris, Miss Winter Park, '59; and Nancy Lundy, Miss Florida, '59 - came on stage wearing fashions from Ivey's.

Mrs. Arnold J. Wilson, Jr. continued her "Art of Listening" lecture series, acquainting her listeners prior to each Subscription Series concert with the programs they were to hear.

The POPS Concerts brought to Orlando guest stars Carmen Cavallero, in January; the Arbors, a vocal quartet, in February; duo-pianists Mr. and Mrs. Leonard Mastrogiacomo in March; and - adding a fourth concert this year - "From Bach to Broadway" music in April, featuring the full Florida Symphony.

On February 7, the Opera Gala Guild and the Junior League of Orlando entertained in the plush Granada Room of the Park Plaza Hotel, where guests mingled with opera stars Beverly Sills, Placido Domingo, Norman Treigle, Dominic Cossa, and Kay Creed, all in town for the February 9 and 11 presentations of Gounod's "Faust". As it happened, the great Beverly Sills and the handsome young Placido Domingo [who had made his debut at the Met in 1969 in the Don Rodrigo role] were actually 'replacements' for two of the originally-scheduled stars who were unable, because of illness, to fulfill their

65

commitments. All last-minute schedule problems should turn out so happily!

During this season, Central Florida - after long study and discussion - finally approved the organization of "The Council of Arts & Sciences of Central Florida". The Council was sponsored by the Florida Symphony Orchestra, the Loch Haven Art Center, Central Florida Museum and Planetarium, Orlando Players Little Theatre, and Rollins College.

This organization was suggested by the Orlando Area Chamber of Commerce's Cultural Affairs Committee for the purpose of coordination, promotion and development of cultural activities in the area. It was hoped that the Arts Council would minimize confusion and overlapping in schedules for performances and exhibits, and would develop a coordinated calendar of programs and events to be mailed free of charge to everyone requesting the information.

Reflecting, perhaps, this concerted effort of cooperation among arts organizations, a new concept in simultaneous fund-raising, for several worthwhile organizations, was introduced to Orlando in 1967. It was a sort of United Appeal for 'culture', and it was called PESO — the name standing for "Participation Enriches Science, Music and Arts Organizations." Chartered as a non-profit organization, its beneficiaries were designated as the Florida Symphony Orchestra, Loch Haven Art Center, John Young Museum and Planetarium, Central Florida Civic Theatre, and the newly-organized Council of Arts & Sciences. PESO instantly became the 'in' thing to support.

PESO's activities were officially launched in early 1968, when spectacular "Prelude to PESO" dinner parties brought out the monied folk and brought in the money. One person described one of these parties thus: "It was a Broadway opening night, the first performance at Lincoln Center, and dinner at The Four Seasons, rolled into one big, exciting evening!"

Capping the climax was the 'really big' PESO Dinner-Auction at Exposition Hall in March, when such fabulous items as antique furniture, a fishing trip for two in Bimini, a duck-hunting trip for two in Yucatan, a complete wardrobe of high-styled clothes, a football flight for fifteen people to a University of Florida football game, and even beautiful new homes, were auctioned to the highest bidder.

It was during this season, too, that the Women's Committee sponsored the publication of "The Florida Heritage Cookbook", containing authentic Florida recipes for everything from soup to nuts — literally! — and then some. Joyce Vickers and Shyla Reich were editors of the publication, and they collected recipes from every source they could find to make their compilation as definitively complete as possible. "The Florida Heritage Cookbook" is now [in 1975] in its second printing, and hundreds of copies have been sold, with all proceeds benefitting the Florida Symphony.

The orchestra was working hard, not only to match the Ford half-million, but to meet its own operating costs each year. It wasn't an easy task. In March, 1968, the famous Philadelphia Symphony Orchestra, more than 100 musicians strong, with conductor, Eugene Ormandy, appeared in Orlando in a special concert, the proceeds of which helped the Florida Symphony in its fund-raising marathon. The Philadelphia Orchestra presented a tremendously thrilling concert, which was received with great appreciation by the packed audience.

> There is no truth obtainable
> By man, than comes of music.
>
> — Robert Browning

Cold weather didn't daunt some 200 music-lovers who went to the Orlando Sports Stadium in late February to hear the first "Dollar Concert Family Night" presented by the Florida Symphony. The presentation was sponsored by the Sentinel-Star Company to benefit the newspaper's 'Shoes for the Shoeless' fund. Those who braved the bitter cold enjoyed the concert. The music was familiar, big, and exciting. Especially appreciated was the appearance of the Jones High School Concert Choir of 75 voices, under the direction of Mrs. Edna Hargrett. Swaying arrangements of tunes like "If I Loved You", "Sit Down Servant", and "Italian Street Song" [featuring a stunning solo by 16-year-old Diana Porter] made the audience forget the weather. The warmth of Curtis Rayam's velvety solo voice also helped in that regard.

Assorted social events crowded the 1967-68 calendar. Following the season's opening concert, an invitation was extended to the entire audience to attend a reception afterward, for the orchestra's new conductor, Hermann Herz, and his charming wife, Lottie. The reception was held in Exposition Hall, adjacent to the Auditorium, and was sponsored by the hard-working Women's Committee.

On March 11, 1968, Mr. & Mrs. Foster David Streep, Jr., were hosts at a reception at their home on Virginia Drive, honoring Miss Helen Ryan, Executive Vice-President of the Florida Symphony Society, Inc., in recognition of her enormous contribution to the growth of the orchestra through all the years of its existance.

Funny things were always happening in the progress of the

orchestra, along with all the hard work. During opera rehearsals for "Faust", lovely Beverly Sills was sitting in a box out front, watching the proceedings, when a mouse ran up her dress! Miss Sills, a great lady whose sense of humor has survived a variety of untoward events, took it all in stride. [Actually, she took large strides to the East, while the mouse scampered off to the West.] Her hosts were embarrassed to no end. Miss Sills thought it was hilarious. The mouse, on the other hand, has become quite a devotee of good music, and was last seen in attendance at the symphony's opening concert in December of 1974.

The Florida Symphony's nineteenth season opened, appropriately enough, on December 19 — with a Christmas-theme concert featuring vocalists from New York backed by the Camerata Chorus under the direction of William Hardy.

Though nobody's crystal ball could see the importance of the event at that time, one 'orchestra promotion' of 1968-69 deserves note. Pavle Despalj, in his second season as violinist with the orchestra, was appointed Associate Conductor for the coming year. Somebody 'upstairs' must have been looking out for the Florida Symphony Orchestra.

Beverly Sills, Soprano

Eight Subscription concerts were scheduled for 1968-69, still in the Orlando Municipal Auditorium. The Children's Series presented "Magic With the Orchestra" in January, the Ballet Royal in February, and a children's opera based on "Jack and the Beanstalk" in April.

The Women's Committee now had a membership of 600, and at a Membership Coffee in May, tables with exhibits and displays acquainted new members with the many ways they could help the symphony. Entertainment was provided by a Style Show, with models wearing up-to-the-minute fashions from John Stephens of 'Carnaby Street' on Park Avenue, Winter Park.

Shyla Reich and Joyce Vickers, editors of the Florida Heritage

Cookbook, which had been published the previous fall as a fund-raising project for the symphony, were hostesses at a Celebration Luncheon at Dubsdread Country Club, to thank all of the editors who worked with them on this eminently successful undertaking. History does not record whether the food served was prepared by Heritage Cookbook recipes, but we'd like to think it was!

"Prelude to PESO" dinner parties were again popular occasions in 1968-69. Hostesses vied among themselves to come up with original party themes, and "Prelude" dinners ranged from formal-candlelight to cookouts on the beach.

The Orlando Bridge Club gave a benefit party for the orchestra in November of 1968, encouraged, no doubt, by Maestro Hermann Herz, who was a bridge enthusiast and a member of the Club.

The annual benefit Fashion Show sponsored by the Women's Committee was also held in November at the Park Plaza Hotel. "Contemp California" was the theme, and Jordan Marsh furnished the mouth-watering cruisewear fashions.

A group called the 'Camerata Chorus' had evolved from the vocalists gathered by Bill Hardy six years previously to provide the chorus for the annual Opera Gala. The Camerata now filled many concert dates of their own, and continued to rehearse diligently year-round.

Camerata Chorus circa 1969

The Symphony Ball date was changed to December this year, in order to get the season's events launched in a spirited and festive way. The Ball, with the theme of "Winter Wonderland", was staged in an elaborately-decorated Exposition Hall. The Florida Symphony, as usual, played during the early hours, followed by Vincent Lopez and his popular orchestra for the remainder of the evening.

The Florida Symphony Orchestra had now been expanded to 75 musicians, enlarging its sound and effectiveness. Since many of the musicians had been drawn from some of the nation's most prestigious orchestras, they were often featured as soloists.

The first 'Christmas POPS' Concert featured the Jones High School Concert Choir with the orchestra, in a program of holiday music. It was a smashing success, as was the Opera Gala Guild's production, that season, of the fully-staged opera, "Tosca". Headlining the "Tosca" cast were Gabriella Tucci, Nicholas Di Virgilia, and the Canadian baritone with the single name of Quilico.

One truly different 'extra' program presented in January, 1970, was called an "Evening In Space". Fabulous photographs of space, in brilliant colors, were flashed on a huge screen [photos were taken by Apollo II astronauts, and loaned for the occasion by NASA] while the symphony played musical terrestrial journeyings. Included on the program were such selections as Gustav Holst's "The Planets", a fantastic number; big-band arranger Ralph Flannigan's "Overture: Rocket to the Moon"; and, naturally, Hoagy Carmichael's "Stardust".

An exhibit of various space items — space suits, a Lunar module, a six-foot model of Saturn V, a fiberglass topographic model of the Ocean of Storms, and other objects, were on display, and were eagerly inspected by the audience. The program was jointly sponsored by Sentinel-Star Charities and Central Florida Museum and Planetarium, who wisely took advantage of the nation's epidemic of 'space fever' to mount an exceptional show that had the town talking for days afterward. They even remembered the ushers, who wore fetching 'Moon Maid' costumes. And they remembered Pavle Despalj, Associate Conductor of the orchestra, who conducted that evening.

Social events continued apace. The Women's Committee's fall luncheon was held in November, honoring charter members of the Committee. The Symphony Ball for the 20th season was a special observance, and as such was jointly sponsored by the Associate Board, the Florida Symphony Society Board of Directors, the Women's Committee, and the Opera Gala Guild. Held December 13 in Exposition Hall, it was, by all estimates, the most opulent Ball ever. The decorating committee performed literal magic by transforming the Hall into an elegant Viennese ballroom, with crystal chandeliers, golden Christmas trees, taffeta-draped pillars and walls, and gold-framed mirrors reflecting the beautiful scene, and the beautiful people.

PESO continued to thrive. Along with the more opulent "Prelude to PESO" dinners were some smaller parties dubbed "PESO Poco" [for those too poor for PESO] and all of them helped swell the PESO fund. Contributions of items to be purchased at the elegant PESO Dinner-Auction became a deluge, with everything from antique bon-bon-dishes to a $65,000 home going on the block. Bidding was so spirited that purchases were still being made at three A.M., but by that time everyone was so caught up in the spirit of the thing that time had been totally forgotten.

Meanwhile, the musicians of the orchestra continued working endlessly to perfect what must be one of the most specialized group activities in existence — the presentation, by 75 separate individuals, of completely-coordinated music. Conductor Herz worked with a definite plan, and always carried it out. There never was a chance element. His conducting style was very broad, and sometimes even overemphasized. He was not only an immaculate and stylish dresser, but he loved to talk. He would narrate anecdotes during a rehearsal, telling of his experiences, or the story behind a composition or about a composer. This was, of course, time consuming. Some of the musicians, who wanted to get down to the business of rehearsal, would get impatient; but, in spite of themselves, they learned a lot from Herz. He was a very genial and warm-hearted person.

Maestro Herz completed his three-year contract with the Florida Symphony during its 20th season, and did not sign another. He elected to return to his former home in Minnesota, where he had accepted the post of Conductor of College and City Orchestras at Mankato, Minnesota, State College. He was also to teach music courses and produce an opera for the college.

Once more, the Florida Symphony needed a new hand at the helm. This time, one was waiting in the wings.

At their meeting in March, 1970, the Florida Symphony Society appointed Pavle Despalj, who had then been Associate Conductor for the previous two seasons, as Music Director and Conductor of the Florida Symphony Orchestra. It was one of the most fortuitous decisions made during the Society's twenty years of existence.

As the Florida Symphony looks to the future, the musical interests and education of our young people will continue to be of primary importance.

GROWING TOWARD TOMORROW
PVALE DESPALJ TO THE PRESENT

For music [which is earnest of a heaven,
seeing we know emotions strange by it,
*   not else to be revealed], is like a voice,*
a low voice calling fancy, as a friend,
*   to the green woods in the gay summertime.*

— *Robert Browning*

Pavle Despalj

Pavle Despalj, the Florida Symphony's new conductor, planned an impressive program for the 21st season.

Despalj [Des-pahl] became a member of the orchestra in the fall of 1967, soon after his arrival in the United States from Yugoslavia. A conductor, composer, violinist, and violist, Mr. Despalj was born in Yugoslavia in 1934, and studied music first under his father. He graduated from Zagreb Music Conservatory in 1955, and the Music Academy in 1960, where he later taught composition.

As conductor, Mr. Despalj appeared with the Zagreb Opera and Symphony Orchestras, the Zagreb Ballet and Chamber Orchestras, and personally founded both the Zagreb Chamber Orchestra and the Belgrade Chamber Orchestra. His compositions have been performed in Yugoslavia, German, Italy, and — now — Orlando, Florida, U.S.A., and have been written for full orchestra, chamber orchestra, and string quartet.

Maestro Despalj's wife, the former Majda Radic, a skilled professional mezzo-soprano, won all hearts with her American operatic debut in the Opera Gala's production of "Rigoletto" in January, 1972. The Maestro's brother, Valter, a professional 'Cellist, studied at Julliard and spent some years in New York, but is now performing in his native country. Pavle's sister, Maja, is a concert violinist in Zagreb, and the first woman to become Concertmaster of a major orchestra in all of Yugoslavia's musical history!

The Florida Symphony's 21st season opened on December 17, 1970, with its exciting new conductor, and an all-Beethoven program featuring Alphonse Carlo, concertmaster, as soloist. Following concerts were marked with both great talents and much diversity.

All music is what awakes from you
When you are reminded by the instruments.

— Walt Whitman

In rapid succession, three young and highly-acclaimed artists appeared as guest soloists — Lorin Hollander, pianist; Majda Despalj, mezzo-soprano; and Itzhak Perlman, Israeli violinist. Cecil Leeson, famed saxophonist, flew here to be guest soloist for the American premiere of Maestro Despalj's own composition, "Concerto for Saxophone". The great lady of the piano, Lili Kraus, appeared with the orchestra that season, as did Arpad Szomoru, the symphony's Principal 'Cellist.

Diversity continued through the 1971 POPS Concerts, which spotlighted the U.S. Air Force 'Singing Sergeants'; Doc Severinson, trumpeter; Vonda Kay Van Dyke, vocalist and former Miss America; and Craig Hundley, a truly smashing teenage jazz pianist.

The Children's Series included an 'introduction-to-the-orchestra' program titled "Magic of Music"; Stravinsky's "The Firebird", danced by the Ballet Royal; and "The Barking Pussycat", an original opera by two University of South Florida graduate students, Ray Holton and Nancy Wetmore.

Two great friends of the Florida Symphony came to Orlando in 1971 specifically to play benefit performances for the orchestra. Artur Rubinstein, legendary piano virtuoso, made one of his rare appearances here on February 12, demonstrating to an appreciative, capacity audience once again the power and beauty of his playing.

Lili Kraus, who had been a guest soloist earlier in the year, offered to come back for a truly special benefit program on May 25. "This

orchestra must have the financial support it needs to maintain its artistic level of performance. I will volunteer to come back to play a benefit concert for your Ford Foundation Matching Fund", she said.

Madame Kraus, internationally known concert pianist, is generally considered by critics to be one of today's outstanding interpreters of Mozart. Her all-Mozart concert featured two of his best-loved Concertos — the E-Flat Major and the D Minor. We are grateful that Lili loved us. Central Florida audiences loved her equally, in return.

Lili Kraus

In November, 1970, F. D. Streep, Jr., President of the Symphony Society, announced that the Society had received a $15,000 grant, earmarked for the Youth Education program. He made it clear, however, that this was separate and apart from the Ford Foundation Fund Grant, so symphony workers continued with their task of raising matching funds to meet the July, 1971 deadline set by the Ford Foundation.

Other arts organizations were not forgotten, even in the midst of the 'Ford years'. The symphony played a benefit in January, 1971, for the Central Florida Museum, under the sponsorship of Sentinel-Star Charities. The program featured the world-famous flamenco guitarist, Carlos Montoya, and was appropriately titled, "Bravo, Montoya!".

Social events continued to flourish. Mr. and Mrs. F. D. Streep, Jr., hosted a Christmas reception honoring the new conductor, Pavle Despalj, and Mrs. Despalj. Guests, who were members of the Symphony Society Board and its hard-working Arms, were delighted to have this chance to begin getting to know the soft-spoken Despaljs. Though Majda was still somewhat unsure of her English, her warm personality and radiant smile bridged all communication barriers.

'Prelude to PESO' parties, in all sizes and shapes, seemed to have caught the accelerated fund-raising fever, and a great crowd was on hand for the PESO Dinner-Auction in Exposition Hall on March 20, 1971. No wonder! One of the prizes to be auctioned was a Texas Oil Well!

In addition to the annual PESO Gala Dinner Auction, a new fund-raising project was instituted by PESO — a two-day TV Auction. Thanks to the public-spirited Board of Directors of WFTV-Channel 9, and General Manager Walter Windsor in particular, the marathon two-day Television Auction sold everything from real estate to condominiums; from antiques to radios; from art to home appliances; even children's toys and real live puppies.

The TV Auction more than doubled PESO's fund-raising capability, and has been an integral part of the PESO Auction activity ever since. Naturally, the mechanics of running both a Gala Dinner Auction and a two-day TV Auction require volunteer workers by the dozen — perhaps by the hundred! The Florida Symphony is extermely grateful for PESO's activities, and would like — here and now — to publicly thank not only those who have volunteered their services in PESO's behalf, but Executive Director Martin Lechner, also, for a job well done.

Caught up in the spirit of expansion — somehow, it seemed to be catching — the Opera Gala Guild, for the first time, presented not one but two fully-staged operas in 1971. February's production of Puccini's

76

"Manon Lescaut" starred Central Florida's favorite, Richard Tucker, together with Raina Kabaivanska, Frank Guarrera, and Andrea Velis — who so charmed those he met that he soon joined Tucker's virtual 'favorite son' category.

The April opera presentation was another 'first' for the busy Opera Gala Guild — the first American opera to be presented in Central Florida. "Susannah", written by Carlisle Floyd, then a member of the Music faculty at Florida State University, was a landmark undertaking, and was also exceptionally well-received. Starring Phyllis Curtin and Norman Treigle, both of whom had also starred in the New York City Opera's debut performance of the work, "Susannah" boasted its author as Stage Director, insuring, in the process, possibly the most 'authentic' production in the Opera Gala Guild's history of authenticity.

Months passed too quickly. The sun rose, the soft winds blew, and suddenly it was June 30, 1971 — a great time to be alive, and 'matched'! Yes, the Florida Symphony Orchestra's many friends had come through like the proverbial 'match-maker', and the marvelous matching $500,000 for the Ford Foundation Grant was now in Trust. You may read the story of those cliff-hanging last days of the campaign under the special chapter on the Ford Foundation Trust elsewhere in this publication. Suffice it to say the trite, "You had to be there", to really know how many fingernails were gnawed off up to the elbow before the final surge of triumph.

Stephen T. Dean, new Symphony Society President, had this to say about the success achieved:

"There are so many people who have contributed to this victory that it would be impossible to name them all."

"Not only have the various committees within the Florida Symphony Society worked hard to achieve this result, but so have other cultural organizations."

"The children of the schools worked hard, and contributed their portion. The business community has worked hard and contributed. The banks have been most faithful, and without them we could not have achieved this result."

"Certainly this victory could not have been celebrated without the great help from the news media. Not only did they contribute money, but they contributed needed publicity."

"Of course, great credit must be given those who have worked within the Symphony organization."

In July, 1971, the Symphony's Board of Directors made a few policy changes. The Arms of the Symphony were officially given separate authority and responsibility, and the Florida Symphony office was to provide only administrative support to each of these organizations. Robert L. Landers was designated Assistant Manager and Administrative Director, responsible for providing such support to these separate organizations within the Symphony Society.

The Women's Committee was officially given responsibility for the POPS Concerts, the Florida Youth Orchestra, and the annual Fashion Show. Members expected to be called upon for symphony fundraising, when needed.

The Associate Board was assigned responsibility for the Children's Concert Series and the Symphony Ball, their traditional functions.

The Opera Gala Guild received the obvious responsibility of presenting the annual Opera, with all the attendant details, including social functions, when desired.

In addition, Board members were given certain fields of responsibility. The orchestra's range of service was 'growing like Topsy', and its supporters accepted their new duties happily.

Its 22nd season saw the Florida Symphony presenting, again, an eight-concert Subscription Series studded with guest artists. As for the 4-concert POPS Series, with such stars as Pete Fountain and his Orchestra, the George Shearing Quintet, pianist Errol Garner, and vocalist Sarah Vaughn, there was surely an artist, somewhere during the season, to fulfill anybody's desires.

The season had been extended to 22 weeks, and still each week was crowded to capacity. The Children's Series, a dozen Orlando Youth Concerts, out-of-town concerts in nine Florida cities, various benefits, the Bach Festival, the Rollins Series, all vied with Orlando and Daytona Subscription Concerts for rehearsal time. "Have instruments, will travel," became a by-word, because the orchestra musicians spent so much time on the road. The symphony had received a $20,000 grant from the National Endowment for the Arts to provide a two-week expansion of its Youth Education Program, so more out-of-town Youth Concerts were added, with delight, to the schedule.

The Opera Gala Guild continued with the two-opera season it had inaugurated in 1971, offering Verdi's "Rigoletto" in January, 1972, and Donizetti's "Lucia di Lammermoor" in April. The former starred Joy Clements, John Macurdy, Leo Goeke, and Frank Guarrera, while "Lucia" brought the lovely Gail Robinson, Dominic Cossa, Robert Moulson, and Peter Harrower to town. Two operas per season meant twice as much work for the Opera Guild membership, but their enthusiasm carried them through with energy to spare.

With the collaboration of the Jones High School Chorus, the orchestra gave an admission-free concert, included in the "Orlando Presents" series, [co-sponsored by the Sentinel-Star Company and the

78

City of Orlando], in December, 1971. The Florida Symphony truly wanted to express its appreciation to all who gave support during the Ford Matching Fund Drive. The "thank you" concert was held in the 3,000-seat Municipal Auditorium, and every seat was filled. Time-honored Christmas Carols were never sung with greater joy, or accompanied by happier musicians.

The Symphony Ball this year was held on February 26, at the fabulous Contemporary Hotel, Walt Disney World - the first time this adjacent wonderland had been available for the Ball. A record crowd exclaimed over the awe-inspiring surroundings, waltzed to the music of the Florida Symphony Orchestra, and danced til the wee hours to the more contemporary rhythms of Jim Downing and the Renegade Brass.

To launch the orchestra's 23rd season, Orlando's Mayor Carl Langford proclaimed the week of December 3, 1972, as "Symphony Week", with the slogan, "Share the Magic of Music". In truth, the growth of the orchestra had been a community happening. From a small group of mostly volunteer musicians, with a $30,000 annual budget, the Florida Symphony had evolved into an outstanding Metropolitan Orchestra of 75 professional musicians - whose scrap books bulged with favorable comments from music critics, many of them nationally-known — and whose 1972-73 budget stood at more than $462,000.

Many people had come to agree with what one critic had written; "The Florida Symphony Orchestra is Central Florida's greatest cultural asset." The fact that the orchestra's budget in 1972-73 was over fifteen times the size of the 1950-51 budget was not only an indication of the growing excellence of the orchestra, but also of the growing acceptance by the people. The money, so difficult to raise, was coming back to the people in a magnificent flood of great music.

The previous December's Christmas concert, under the auspices of the "Orlando Presents" series, had been such a hit that another was scheduled for Sunday afternoon, December 10, 1972. Entitled "Cavalcade of Music", it presented a host of 'local' talent, including Mariachi Chaparral and the Dapper Dan Quartet, both from Walt Disney World: Choirs from Florida Technological University and Valencia Community College: two Sweet Adeline Quartets: Ralph Eyman on the classical guitar, and Gene Holm on string bass.

As the orchestra's budget became larger and larger, new income sources were constantly being sought. One which was originated this season, and which has proved popular ever since, was 'selling' the sponsorship of individual concerts. The sponsoring firm receives recognition at 'their' concert, plus certain space in the concert program, in return for a sizeable contribution to the orchestra. Eastern Air Lines 'premiered' this procedure, by sponsoring the first POPS Concert of the 1972-73 season. The Lionel Hampton Band was the stellar attraction, and this lively and jumping group rocked right into the hearts of the full-house audience. Whatever Hamp can't do with a set of vibes is better off not done, anyway - and his 'specialists' on drums, piano, Congas, saxophones and trumpets were all star-quality in their own right.

This season the orchestra tried adding something new to its schedule and came a cropper. Three 'Promenade' concerts were scheduled, to be held at Winter Park High School Auditorium on Sunday afternoons. The music was to be light — and beautiful music for a beautiful Sunday afternoon sounded like a sure-fire bet. The first 'Promenade' concert was an all-Gershwin program, presenting F.T.U.'s Dr. Gary Wolf, pianist, playing "Concerto in F"; the Jones High School Concert Choir singing excerpts from "Porgy and Bess"; and solo vocals by Bill Jones, baritone, and Irene Wild, soprano. Despite the convenient time, and the popular program, very few were in the audience.

The second 'Promenade' offering was a potpourri of lilting Viennese music, normally tremendously popular, but again — very few were in the audience. So few, in fact, that the third scheduled 'Promenade' concert was cancelled entirely. Nobody could explain why the theoretically 'ideal' conditions hadn't jelled, but orchestra management was forced to abandon that idea, and look for others.

The eight-concert Subscription Series was star-studded, by any standards, with the brightest star being the incomparable Leontyne Price, soprano, in her first Orlando appearance. Madame Price is very selective about the concert engagements which she elects to accept, and her decision to join the Florida Symphony in concert was a compliment to both conductor and musicians.

Lili Kraus, always an Orlando favorite, also appeared during the 1972-73 season, as did the famed Philadelphia Orchestra under the baton of Eugene Ormandy.

The Florida Symphony's out-of-town schedule this season included not only the six Subscription concerts in Daytona Beach, but appearances in Lake City, Marianna, Madison, Valdosta, [Georgia], Mount Dora, Leesburg, Fort Pierce, Lakeland, Sanford, Kissimmee, Gainesville, Winter Haven, Melbourne, Eustis and West Palm Beach.

Maestro Pavle Despalj continued to win friends and admirers as Music Director/Conductor of the Florida Symphony. He also had the friendship and confidence of his musicians in the orchestra. One member of the orchestra said: "He is a most artistic person, which comes to the foreground in his conducting. He is always interested in the finest details, and is able to carry this out no matter how large or small the musical canvas. His taste for musical coloring is most varied and refined and he is able to manipulate the orchestra to achieve his desired results."

The Opera Gala Guild, now accustomed to double productions each season, presented a 'Puccini Festival', with "LaBoheme" in February and "La Rondine" in March. "La Boheme" starred Dominic Cossa, of the Metropolitan Opera, and Patricia Craig, rising young star of the New York Opera Company, while "La Rondine" featured Joy Clements, Leo Goeke, and Joanne Yockey, all of New York.

The Women's Committee's annual fashion show this year was called "Fall Fantasy", and took the form of a champagne brunch held in October, in the lovely gardens of the Charles O. Andrews, Jr., home in Winter Park. Fashions from Proctor's previewed the fall and winter season. Another special event benefitting the orchestra was the Winter Park Junior Service League's usual party, this season dubbed "A Night In Rio", held — appropriately enough — at Rio Pinar Country Club.

In the spring of 1973, as the orchestra looked toward its 24th season, Miss Helen Ryan resigned the office of Executive Vice-President to devote her full attention to managing 'her' orchestra. Miss Ryan had been deeply involved in all phases of the work of the Florida Symphony since its inception in 1950. She had served as President of the Symphony Society for seven years, and as Executive Vice President and General Manager for thirteen years. At all times she had been an inspired fund-raiser, and her dedication had provided stability through many uncertain moments.

Robert L. Landers, Assistant General Manager of the orchestra since 1969, was named to succeed Miss Ryan as Executive Vice-president and General Manager. The phenomenal growth of the Florida Symphony truly required two strong hands at the helm, and both Robert Landers and Helen Ryan looked forward to the myriad details, events — and, yes, problems — of the now-23 week season coming up.

Even this latest extension of the season didn't seem to relieve the frantic pace. The Subscription series was also expanded, to nine concerts, and with the Daytona Beach six-concert Series, POPS Concerts, Children's Concerts, Youth Concerts by the dozen, and out-of-town concerts in fifteen Florida cities, there was no time for rest. For the first time, the Florida Symphony was invited to perform in Miami Beach, in a concert featuring the popular gentlemen from the Met, Richard Tucker and Robert Merrill. The amalgamation of talents was a happy one, and both stars and symphony were warmly received by a packed house.

Out-of-town dates which don't require overnight stays are called 'run outs' by the musicians. Once, during the 1973-74 season, a 'run out' turned into a 'run back'. When the orchestra arrived for a concert in Mount Dora, it was discovered that music for the second half of the concert had somehow been left in other folders back in the library in Orlando.

A rather rapid and harrowing drive back to Orlando ensued immediately. The breathless librarian returned to set out the formerly-missing music just as the musicians were going onstage for the second half of the Mount Dora concert. The audience never knew that they came very close to hearing the first half of that concert twice!

The Children's Series for the 24th season included the now-standard all-orchestra concert, a ballet performance featuring Kip Watson's dancers from the School for the Performing Arts, and a choral production in which the Valencia Community College Choir was featured. The series this year was underwritten by Leonard L. Farber, on behalf of Fashion Square, and all concerts were free to the children attending.

This season, also, the orchestra gave a spate of special concerts: four were at Walt Disney World [one with guest soloist Marguerite Piazza], and two at Floida Technological University, during their Festival of Contemporary Music. Gary Wolf, pianist, and Sabina Micarelli, violinist, appeared as soloists during these Contemporary Music concerts. Finally, the Sentinel-Star Charities concert [to benefit the Florida Symphony] presented New York City Ballet's incomparable Edward Villella and Violette Verdy, who played to as enthusiastic an audience as Municipal Auditorium had seen in many a day.

The orchestra again participated in the annual Bach Festival in February-March at Rollins College, and was included on the Rollins Series with four concerts during the months of January through April.

In December of 1973 the Florida Symphony for the first time took over sponsorship of the Ballet Royal-Florida Symphony holiday production of the traditional ballet, "The Nutcracker". Symphony management felt that if virtually every other city in the United States was assured this annual event, Orlando should be no exception. So dance joined the Bach Festival, the Rollins Series, "Orlando Presents", benefits, youth education, and other on-going projects as an integral part of the orchestra's ever-growing contribution to the cultural climate of Central Florida.

The "Orlando Presents" concert in the spring of 1974 was held at the Lake Eola Bandshell, in the closing days of a packed season during which — by a miracle — not one single sheet of music had been lost. But, as luck would have it, during that concert two rather expensive

82

first Violin parts were caught up by a gentle zephyr and wafted straight into the lake!

Since the inception of PESO, the Florida Symphony has, each year, donated a concert to be sold at the Dinner Auction. And, each year, it has been purchased by the Sentinel-Star Company, and presented at no charge to those attending. This season, the PESO concert was held at 2:30 P.M. on April 21, with Irene Wild, soprano; William Jones, baritone; Tom Brockman, pianist; and the Camerata Chorus and choirs from Florida Technological University and Rollins College. The program was all-Gershwin, and the capacity audience in Municipal Auditorium was all-enthusiastic.

The 24th season included twenty-seven out-of-town Youth Concerts, while in Orange County the energy crisis forced substitution of in-school concerts [by split orchestra] for the traditional Youth Concerts in Municipal Auditorium. Some 80 in-school concerts by Florida Symphony performing groups met with such success that requests were made to continue them in future years, when possible, in addition to the large full-orchestra Youth Concerts. It was one more proof that many clouds have pure silver linings.

The 1973-74 POPS Series featured again Pete Fountain and his Band, playing Pete's own New Orleans jazz, followed by the rather 'rock-y' group, "Impact of Brass", comedienne Phyllis Diller — who actually played piano with the orchestra, and rather well, at that — and the Charlie Byrd Trio. Maestro Despalj broke up the orchestra during the Diller rehersal when she pointed out something in the script to him, and he urbanely replied, "Oh, yes, I know what I'm supposed to do. But is it okay if I improvise a little?"

This was also the year that Richard Tucker made his final guest appearance with the Florida Symphony. Together with Robert Merrill, he had thrilled a full house in a March concert, and had spoken, warmly — as always — about the excellence of the orchestra. Orlando had taken Richard Tucker to its heart in 1958, when he appeared in the first Opera Gala in Concert form, and had welcomed him back repeatedly through the years. His untimely death in early 1975 saddened his friends the world over, including a host in Central Florida.

Richard Tucker

83

The Opera Gala Guild elected to put its energies into only one opera for the 1973-74 season, but went all-out to please its audience with Donizetti's rollicking "Daughter of the Regiment". Five stars — Gail Robinson, Arnold Voketaetis, Andrea Velis, William McDonald, and Jean Kraft — under the direction of Patrick Tavernia, of the Metropolitan Opera Company — mounted one of the gayest operas in the Guild's history. The 'Regiment' marched down the aisles of the auditorium, drums rolling, and the audience felt they were truly a part of the production.

Warren R. Winn, Jr., was president of the Floida Symphony Society, Inc. during the eventful 24th season, succeeding Stephen T. Dean. Although Mr. Winn served only one year, his interest in the symphony is of long standing, and has in no way diminished since his relinquishing the position of President. Hugh J. Jones, Jr. was elected to the Presidency to guide the orchestra through its gala 25th season.

Now, in 1975, the Florida Symphony Orchestra — to the amazement of some and the delight of thousands — is celebrating its Silver Anniversary. And there is much to celebrate: most of all, the orchestra itself, which is not only alive and well, but ranks among the finest symphony orchestras in the country.

Although the Florida Symphony has been fully-professional for twenty-two years, and its musicians have been dedicated as well as professional, it hasn't been an easy road. For a long time, the orchestra's limited season made it difficult to attract and hold first-rate personnel who needed a longer working season. But, as the orchestra's season lengthened, and its prestige grew, it was able to attract increasingly excellent musicians, experienced with major orchestras such as Boston, Philadelphia, New York, and Chicago. Presently, the top talent for each vacancy is screened by a stringent Audition Committee — and their work is cut out for them. As an example of the Florida Symphony's drawing power among musicians, last season there were 26 applicants for one opening [Assistant Principal] in the trumpet section.

Far from least of the reasons that the Florida Symphony has achieved its present position has been the quality of its Conductors. Chardon, Miller, Mazer, Herz and Despalj — each had outstanding training in his profession, and has given excellent leadership in the way, and at the time, that it was needed. Each Conductor, in his own way, from his own unique knowledge and his own imaginative approach to music, has provided the orchestra with interest, dedication, and growth. From the lofty vantage of twenty-five years, one applauds, with astonishment, the exceptional foresight of past Florida Symphony Society Boards, who acted upon both the

84

information at hand and their 'instinct' about the orchestra. Their cumulative 'batting average' has been fantastic.

Pavle Despalj, now enjoying his fifth season as Conductor and Music Director of the Florida Symphony, has an enviable reputation both in this country and abroad. An American citizen since January, 1974, his first position in the United States was typical of his constant search for adding to his musical knowledge. He joined the Radio City Music Hall Orchestra, to gain more experience with popular American music. Shortly thereafter, a fellow Yugoslav, who was playing with the Florida Symphony, suggested that Pavle might like to join the orchestra. He came to Orlando, was auditioned, and secured a position as violinist. The following season, he was named Associate Conductor, in which position he served two years, being called upon frequently to conduct the orchestra.

When the position of Music Director/Conductor became vacant, Despalj was the unanimous choice of the Florida Symphony Society Board of Directors. Under his guidance, the orchestra has not only improved dramatically, but has become a polished, assured performing unit, presenting exciting performances, in all musical media, with professional aplomb. Maestro Despalj chooses challenging programs, which his musicians appreciate. He says, "I always try to strike a balance between classical, romantic and contemporary works. I know that music from the Romantic and Post-Romantic periods is more appealing to the audiences — but I also try to promote pieces that I believe deserve public hearing."

Over eighty concerts are scheduled this 25th season, which will tax both Despalj's and the musicians' talents on every front. The season was extended to twenty-five weeks, which seemed appropriate in honor of the orchestra's 25th Anniversary. The local Subscription Series was expanded to ten concerts this anniversary year, with the legendary Leontyne Price, soprano, as guest artist for the opening concert. A double-premiere was the highlight of the January 16, 1975 Subscription Series concert, when the Maestro's sister, Maja Despalj [of Zagreb, Yugoslavia] made her professional American debut, playing her brother's Violin Concerto in its American premiere.

Because of the 25th Anniversary celebration, the Opera Gala Guild decided to make an exceptional choice in the opera to be presented. AIDA, the grandest of all grand operas, requiring the most lavish production ever staged by the Guild, was their selection. Two completely sold-out houses applauded opera stars Jessye Norman, as "Aida", Majda Despalj — who dazzled both audience and critics as "Amneris", Robert Nagy, as "Radames", and McHenry Boatwright as "Amonasro". Patrick Tavernia was again on deck for his most demanding stage directing assignment to date, and the Florida Symphony, under Pavle Despalj, provided splendid support for this mammoth undertaking.

Because of the enormity of the production, the Camerata Chorus was joined by Valencia Community College Chorus [Jean Masterson, director] and the Jones High School Concert Choir [Edna Hargrett, director]. The size of the cast put dressing-room space at a premium, so a large striped 'dressing tent' was erected behind Municipal Auditorium to take care of the overflow.

A double-brace of prominent community leaders were persuaded to act as 'supers' [translate that spear-carriers, banner-wavers, or jewel-chest custodians] and so many male knees have seldom been seen at one time this far west of New Smyrna Beach. Everyone involved in AIDA became so caught up in the momentum of the project that the let-down, once the 'impossible' had been so gloriously achieved, was shattering. But AIDA had indeed arrived in splendor, and had also silenced the pessimists who had said 'You'll never be able to do it!'

In order to finance AIDA, the Opera Gala Guild in 1974 came up with a brand-new idea — the "Decorator Show House" — which was successful beyond their wildest dreams. Professional interior designers in the area cooperated with the Guild by taking one room each of a large, for-sale mansion and bringing the place to brilliant life with their distinctive and divergent ideas. The Guild plans to repeat this successful innovation on a continuing basis. It is hoped that hundreds of people will again happily pay the entrance fee to see the newest in designer planning, the most unusual in hand-made boutique items, and — at the same time — further the presentation of grand opera in Central Florida.

A truly unprecedented event was jointly sponsored in October of 1974 by the Florida Symphony Society and the Central Florida Jewish Community Council. This was the very first Florida appearance of the famed Israel Philharmonic Orchestra. The sought-after young violinist, Pinchas Zukerman, was soloist, and it was evident that his penchant for tennis [he had played the morning of the concert with the Florida Symphony Board's Joe Culp] only served to strengthen his bowing arm. An ecstatic audience gave both Zukerman and the Israel Philharmonic a sustained standing ovation, which they had surely earned. As a sidelight to the Israel Philharmonic's visit to the area — an entire Greyhound busload of their musicians spent a day at, you guessed it, Walt Disney World!

So now, in the year 1975, Central Florida has been fortunate enough to have had its own Floida Symphony Orchestra for 25 years. People, in many multiples of 25, have kept it not only going, but growing, during those years. We feel, also, that people — in even greater multiples of 25 — have both enjoyed the orchestra, and profited from it.

In truth, 'music hath charms...', and the Florida Symphony hopes that at least some of their music has charmed you. Through all the Allegros and the Andantes, the Fortes and the Pianissimos, the Beethoven and the Sousa, the thousands [literally!] of hours of rehearsal, the hundreds of hours in local concerts [and more hundreds of hours on a bus going to present a concert someplace else] the Florida Symphony has been — and is — a phenomenon. Though created, perhaps, by a few — it has been made possible, unquestionably, by many.

If you are reading this book, this is your orchestra. We hope you share, even in small part, our immense pride in this organization and its accomplishments.

EPILOG

L'ENVOI

Have you got a minute? Please!! This is important!

In looking backward through the twenty-five years of the history of the Florida Symphony Orchestra, some truths become selfevident — and NUMBER ONE would be that there are due thanks without number in all directions.

Nobody, no organization, anywhere, anyhow, any time, ever received more local publicity — and gratifying national publicity — than the Florida Symphony Orchestra. The proof is in the stacks and stacks of yard-square scrapbooks, which break the back to lift, but warm the heart to read. Thank you, newspapers, magazines, all the radio and television commentators who sang our praises so glowingly, who praised our efforts AND our results, and never failed to promote our projects.

Thank you, especially, Orlando Sentinel-Star, for having printed enough symphony copy over the years to fill a dozen bookcases, if it could be compiled and bound. Thank you, too, for skilled reviewers who 'told it like it was', and refused to fill our heads with empty praise. When they gave a "Bravo", it was deserved — and treasured!

Thank you famous stars, great personalities, professional musicians, who have shared your talents so generously for our benefit.

Thank you people in Florida and even farther away who have supported the symphony so constructively: the city governments — most especially, the City of Orlando — the state government, the National Endowment for the Arts, the civic clubs, the schools, thousands of invaluable contributors, wonderful PESO, and, most of all, the audiences for our concerts.

Thank you, salaried and volunteer office help, for your time, and overtime, in our cause.

Thank you, Junior League of Orlando, for pioneering, and — by your efforts — giving Central Florida the gift of Grand Opera. Thank you for creating the Opera Gala Guild, for giving the Guild the strength of your hard-earned knowledge, and the determination to tackle ever-growing projects.

Thank you, First National Bank of Orlando, [now Sun First National] for your unfailing faith in us, through the years, and your unhesitating assistance on occassions far too numerous to mention.

Thank you, Ford Foundation Trust Fund, for giving the Florida Symphony Society the opportunity to share in your bounty. By the tremendous effort of many people in many communities we were able to raise $500,000 to match Ford's $500,000 in the five years ending in July, 1971. If the annual financial storms of the following five years [until July, 1976] can be weathered — and, so far, they have been — a somewhat protected harbor will be reached. It will be a comfort to have a one million dollar Trust Fund. But with the symphony budget rapidly approaching a million per year — as beautiful as our million dollars will be, it must grow along with the budget, and must not be eroded by expenditures.

Thank you, music lovers everywhere, for your cooperation, your money to pay the bills, your oft-expressed appreciation for what the symphony has meant to you. Concert-goer Mrs. W. H. Farlinger, 85, is one of these dear-to-our-heart patrons. Mrs. Farlinger has bought a season ticket to the symphony concerts for twenty-four of our twenty-five seasons. She has occupied the same reserved seat for all those years, and has missed only one concert! At the opening concert of the 1974-75 season, Mrs. Farlinger was reminiscing: "I think the current Conductor, Pavle Despalj, is the best we've had", she said.

Thank you, unknown benefactors, whose gifts and support have helped the Florida Symphony Orchestra to grow and prosper. Though you'll read the names, in the Appendix, of many people who have given much to the symphony in time and money, some prefer anonymity. We'd like to give every one a halo, named or not.

It would seem that getting started is the hardest part of any undertaking — that the Florida Symphony Orchestra, now so well-known, so well-established, would find nothing but blue skies from now on.

But, it doesn't always work that way, does it? Inflation, depression, freezes, hurricanes, booms and busts — Florida has experienced them all. They are uninvited guests, but they do come occasionally.

Twenty-five years is a young age, and it is true that the symphony has achieved an unbelievable amount of success in those years. But our dreams for the future are even greater.

By custom, orchestras are 'rated' by the amount of their annual budget. Those with a budget between $500,000 and one million dollars are categorized as 'Metropolitan' Orchestras. With a current budget of $628,000-plus, the Florida Symphony presently falls into this category. Orchestras with a budget of $1,000,000 or more are categorized as

MAJOR Orchestras. This is the direction in which we are headed! But our dream for the Florida Symphony is not simply to become a Major Orchestra by virtue of a million-dollar budget, but to become a Major Orchestra whose performance is equal to any in the country!

> A man that has a taste of
> music, painting or architecture
> is like one that has another sense,
> when compared with such as
> have no relish of those arts.
>
> — Joseph Addison

If our present growth level continues, that is not only a possibility, but a probability, within the next five years. The current economic situation will not last forever, and we believe that Florida, with all it has to offer, will be among the first areas to recover.

Another dream is that soon we will have a Performing Arts Theater of which we can be proud — with good acoustics, comfortable seating, attractive dressing rooms for the stars, adequate rest rooms for the patrons — a Theater not only built for the presentation of the performing arts, but one that is beautiful and restful, properly heated and air-conditioned, easily accessible to the public, with a large, paved parking lot.

A continuing dream is to further lengthen the orchestra's season, making it possible to present more concerts, bring in more great artists, and go on longer tours — so that more people in more places will be able to enjoy the Florida Symphony's music. Many of our musicians are now settling here, since they can count on the longer season we have already achieved. Thirty to thirty-five have bought homes here. Several are teaching in nearby colleges.

Perhaps our biggest dream is that the Florida State Legislature will one day recognize the Florida Symphony as THE FLORIDA Symphony — the orchestra for all of Florida. We feel that the orchestra has already earned the right to such recognition, and deserves the prestige of 'official' status.

> Music washes away from the soul
> the dust of everyday life.
>
> — Auerbach

If you have dreams for the Florida Symphony — share them with us. We're ready and willing to try to attain incredible goals. There's an unquenchable spirit that pervades symphony workers. The list of officers and directors of our parent body, the Florida Symphony Society, and its Arms — the Women's Committee, Associate Board, and Opera Gala Guild — today contains names of many whose parents were on the first list, twenty-five years ago. The parents, now, are probably serving in other capacities, but they are still interested and working.

Theirs is the spirit that perseveres, that does not accept defeat. It's a spirit communicated to new workers for the symphony, and they in turn will pass it along to those that follow. This is only the end of a short era — and the beginning of a new period of growth and achievement. It's a time for bringing new friends into the symphony orbit, so that they, too, will have a part in this magnificent undertaking.

Thank you!

R.G.S.

Dorothy Kirsten and Cesare Valletti rehearse with a chorus comprised of Central Florida singers prior to the Opera Gala in Concert, February, 1960.

THE FLORIDA SYMPHONY SOCIETY PRESIDENTS —

THE MOVERS AND SHAKERS AT THE HELM

We are the music makers,
    And we are the dreamers of dreams,
World-losers and world-forsakers
    On whom the pale moon gleams;
Yet we are the movers and shakers
    Of the world forever, it seems.

                    — Arthur W. E. O'Shaughnessy

Robert S. Carr

ROBERT S. CARR 1950-51

When he shall die
Take him and cut him in little stars,
And he will make the face of heaven so fine
That all the world will be in love with night,
And pay no worship for the garish sun.

— Shakespeare

One of the most civic-minded citizens of Orlando, Robert S. Carr, was the first President of the Florida Symphony Society, Inc.

Before becoming Mayor of Orlando, which office he held for ten years, he was prominent in banking, real estate and mortgage loan brokerage. He served as Secretary-Treasurer and Director of Curtis O'Neal Company, and later the Central Title and Trust Company, as President. He served in that capacity until Central's merger with the Citizens National Bank of Orlando in 1962.

Among Mayor Carr's accomplishments were the construction of the new City Hall, Central Fire Station, Jet Terminal facilities at McCoy, and two successful bond issues.

Mayor Carr assisted Orlando Negro citizens, and helped organize Washington Shores, a non-profit Negro land development project.

Mayor Carr served as president of the Florida League of Municipalities and helped organize such civic groups as Community Chest of Orlando, Orange County Society for Crippled Children, the Florida Symphony Society, Inc., [and in so doing the Florida Symphony Orchestra,] and the Visiting Nurses Association.

Robert S. Carr was a member of the University Club of Orlando and served four terms as its President. He was involved in the building of many other important organizations in the area, and received many honorary awards for his work.

Mr. Carr died suddenly of a heart attack in January, 1967. He had been not only a strong supporter of the Florida Symphony Orchestra since it was organized, but of many projects throughout the area, whose present worth attests to his efforts. His death was a great loss to the thousands who knew him, but his continuing contributions to the good life in Central Florida remain as his memorial.

John G. Baker

JOHN G. BAKER - 1951-52 and 1952-53

John G. Baker, a native of Indiana, came to Orlando in January, 1925. A graduate of Earlham College and University of Indiana Law School, he served as City Attorney for the City of Orlando for approximately twenty years, under four Mayors. He was County Judge for five years.

Judge Baker was one of the principal organizers of the Florida Symphony Society, Inc., and served as the second President of the organization. He was elected to this post for two seasons, and remained as chairman of the Financial Committee for many years.

He has practiced law in Orlando for fifty years, and has been both a member of the Board of Governors of the Florida Bar Association, and President of the Orange County Bar Association. He was a partner in the law firms of Baker & Thornal for twenty-five years, until Justice Campbell Thornal was appointed to the Florida Supreme Court.

Since 1968, Judge Baker has been associated as Counsel with the Orlando office of the law firm of Carleton, Fields, Ward, Emmanuel, Smith & Cutler, one of the oldest law firms in Florida.

Judge Baker has been active in many civic organizations. He served many years on the Board of Governors of Orange Memorial Hospital, and as attorney for the hospital for thirty-five years. He was the first Chairman of the Orlando Human Relations Committee, and served as such for five years. He is a Past President and a lifetime Honorary Member of the University Club.

Through long friendship and association with Senator Spessard Holland, and acting as City Attorney, Judge Baker obtained joint use of McCoy Air Force Base for commercial aviation, and established Orlando as a terminal on the Southern Transcontinental Air Route from Florida to California.

John G. Baker's son, John A. Baker, orgainzed and was the first President of the Associate Board of the Symphony Society.

Judge Baker is married to Jesse Pedrick Baker, well-known organist and pianist.

Helen E. Ryan

MISS HELEN E. RYAN - 1953-54 through 1959-60

*Age cannot wither her
Nor custom stale
Her infinite variety.*

— *Shakespeare*

Miss Helen E. Ryan is a hard one to pin down to any one responsibility, when you're talking about the Florida Symphony Society. She has worked so long and so faithfully in all phases of its growth - organization, fund-raising, hiring personnel, contact with artists, musicians, conductors, public relations - there is nothing she has not done, so dedicated has she been to every phase of the work.

Miss Ryan served as President of the Florida Symphony Society for seven years, starting with the 1953-54 season, and resigning at the end of the 1959-60 season. But, being Helen Ryan, she did not resign her interest. She became Executive Vice-president and General Manager, positions she held for some thirteen years. Two years ago, she felt the need to be able to work more closely with the orchestra and the conductor, so relinquished her executive position to become Orchestra Manager. By this time, the orchestra had grown so much that someone was needed to handle the hundreds of details, relieving the conductor and musicians of that responsibility. Miss Ryan's former positions were taken over by her assistant, Robert L. Landers.

Miss Ryan was born into a musical family in Utica, New York. Her early musical training was with her sister, and later she attended the New England Conservatory of Music, in Boston.

At sixteen, Helen Ryan had her own Orchestra of twenty-five men, and they played engagements throughout Central New York State. She also did a great deal of accompanying, which she enjoyed more than any other phase of music.

In 1932, she decided to become active in something other than music, so she and Joy Hawley bought an establishment called "The Whistling Oyster", in Ogunquit, Maine. It was the oldest gift shop and tea room in Maine, and enjoyed a large patronage of summer people, including many from the theater and music fields, there for summer concerts and summer stock. The "Oyster" became famous nationally, and it seemed that they should have a winter location in the South.

After exploring many places in Florida, they decided that Orlando - then a small city - was where they would enjoy living, and that there was a potential for a really fine shop here. The only thing missing was enough music - but Helen felt something could eventually be done about that.

Naturally, she was interested in helping start a symphony orchestra, and was ready to do whatever she could to help make it go. Fortunately, her partner shared her interest, and didn't mind that Helen had to take a lot of time away from the business to raise money for the orchestra. In fact, Joy Hawley worked hard for the orchestra, too.

After twenty-seven years, Helen & Joy closed the successful Orlando Whistling Oyster Shop - a blow to shoppers here who had grown accustomed to the quality gifts they sold - expecting to concentrate on the Ogunquit "Oyster", which had grown tremendously. But Helen found herself returning to Orlando and the orchestra every Fall. Meanwhile, Joy Hawley, who was in ill health, stayed at home, and continued training their remarkable parakeet, Presto, who was quite a famous bird. He had even appeared on national television, showing off his extensive vocabulary, which Joy - in her precise speaking voice - had taught him.

As a striking example of his prowess, here is a true story. One evening, a motorist lost control of his car on the Boston Turnpike, crossed the median, and hit Miss Ryan's and Miss Hawley's car. Presto was a passenger, and when Joy went with the highway patrolman to get help, Presto went with her. The patrolman nearly had a wreck himself when Presto, with much exasperation, said: "This is a preposterous situation."

Miss Hawley's health grew worse, and she died on August 31, 1964, after a long illness. Following her death, Miss Ryan sold the Ogunquit property and the name, "Whistling Oyster", which was registered in Washington, and she has been in Orlando with the orchestra ever since.

Even though Miss Ryan has announced that she is retiring from working actively with the Florida Symphony Orchestra, her interest and devotion will always be with it, for she is leaving a big part of herself right there.

How will the Florida Symphony get along without her? It is hard to imagine. But a suggestion might be that they find some very loose and comfortable golden chains to put securely around her, so that she cannot get very far away, when we need her so much.

George W. Johnson

GEORGE W. JOHNSON - 1960-61 and 1961-62

George W. Johnson, a native of New Castle, Pa., attended grade schools in New Castle, and his secondary education was received at Sidwell Friends School in Washington, D.C. He received his B.S. degree from Haverford College in 1929, and his LL.B. degree from Harvard University in 1932. He was given an Honorary Doctor of Laws Degree from Rollins College in 1961.

He practiced law in New Castle briefly, and in 1934 moved to Orlando, Florida, where he has practiced law since that time.

He served in the United States Army Air Force, 1942-1946, being honorably discharged with the rank of Major.

In addition to his law practice, Mr. Johnson has been a stockholder, Vice President and director of the Citizens National Bank [now Pan-American Bank] of Orlando since 1947; a stockholder, director and Vice President of the Orange State Bank, Orlando; a stockholder, officer and director of several real estate holding companies; a director and stockholder of the Acceptance Corporation of Florida, an Orlando finance company; managing partner with members of his family in a family investment holding partnership; and has served as "accommodation director" for various corporations represented by his law firm.

Mr. Johnson is a member of the Central Christian Church of Orlando, having served as a Deacon for many years. He was Chairman of the Council Board in 1955 and 1956, and is now serving as Trustee-Deacon.

He has been active in Community Chest and United Appeal drives, serving several times as Chairman of the large gifts Committee.

He has served as a Director of the Orlando Chapter of the American Red Cross, and as Chairman of its annual drive.

In 1939, Mr. Johnson was appointed to the Housing Authority of the City of Orlando, and has served as a member from that date except for his absence in the service during the War. He has been Chairman of the Housing Authority since 1955. He served as President of the Florida Association of Housing Authorities in 1940-1941.

He was principal organizer of the Optimist Club of Orlando and served as its first president in 1940. Prior to World War II, Mr. Johnson served on the Board of Governors of the Orange General Hospital. In 1941-1942 he organized and became the first President of the Central Florida Blood Bank.

He has served as Director of the University Club of Orlando, and was its President in 1942. He served as a Director and Vice President of the Orlando Country Club and as a Director and First Vice-President of the Orlando Chamber of Commerce.

102

In 1946, Mr. Johnson was appointed by the Governor of the State of Florida to serve on the Board of Public Instruction of Orange County. Following his appointment he was elected to two terms on the Board, serving until 1955. He served as Chairman of the Board of Public Instruction from 1949 to 1955. For his service as a member of the Board of Public Instruction, the Junior Chamber of Commerce, in 1953, awarded him the Good Government Award.

He served as a Director of the Florida Symphony Society, Inc. from 1960-1967. He was its President for two years, and Chairman of the Board for the year 1967-68.

Mr. Johnson has served as a member of the Recreation Board of the City of Orlando since 1954, and has been its chairman since 1957. He was a Trustee of the Loch Haven Art Center. Presently he is serving on the Advisory Board of the Florida Sanitarium and Hospital.

He was one of the organizers of Trinity Preparatory School, and is currently serving on its Board in the capacity of Vice-Chairman of the Board. Mr. Johnson has served as Secretary of the Board of Trustees of Rollins College for the past fifteen years, and as a member of Local Draft Board #102 since 1962.

He is a member of Bay Hill Country Club, and served as its President for two years. He was a Charter member of the Central Florida Development Committee, and served on the Board of Directors from its inception in 1959 until 1966. He also served as Vice-President.

Mr. Johnson has been a member of the Committee of 100 of Orange County since its organization in 1956.

Robert T. Anderson

ROBERT T. ANDERSON 1962-63 through 1965-66

Robert T. Anderson served four seasons as President of the Florida Symphony Society, Inc., and it was during his term in office that the Ford Foundation Grant was obtained.

He was a representative at the first Festival of Arts at the White House, Washington, D.C.

A native of Ventura County, California, Mr. Anderson is a graduate of the University of Florida Business Administration and Law Schools. He served as Class President, and was a letterman of the University of Florida football team and a member of the Band.

He is senior partner of the law firm of Anderson & Rush, Orlando. His other business interests include land owner and developer [presently mobile home parks], Director of American Pioneer Life Insurance Company, and Chairman of the Board of American Federal Savings & Loan Association of Orlando. He is a former citrus grower.

A member of the Episcopal Church, Mr. Anderson is past Trustee and past member of the Executive Committee of the Diocese of South Florida, and past member of the Chapter of the Cathedral Church of St. Luke, Orlando. He is a past Trustee of the University of the South, Suwannee, Tennessee, and Attorney and Trustee for Florida Episcopal College.

Mr. Anderson was a Lieutenant Colonel in the Infantry in World War II. He is a graduate of the Command and General Staff College.

He is a Past President of Loch Haven Art Center, member of the Country Club of Orlando, Kiwanis Club and Committee of Two Hundred. His hobbies are the decorative arts.

Mr. Anderson is married to the former Gertrude Johnson, of Orlando. They have a son and daughter, and five grandchildren.

Craig Linton

CRAIG LINTON — 1966-67 and 1967-68

Craig Linton served as President of the Florida Symphony Society, Inc., for two terms — 1966-67, and 1967-68. These were crucial years in the growth of the orchestra, and Mr. Linton exerted a strong stabilizing influence when it was most needed. He inspired confidence, and injected a positive attitude in his relations with both Board and orchestra. Though it must have been an uphill battle most of the way, Craig Linton kept all the programs of the Orchestra moving ahead without a pause.

Mr. Linton, who is a partner in Florida Ranch Lands, Inc., was graduated from Bucknell University with a B.S. in Commerce and Finance. He presently serves as a director of Barnett First National Bank of Winter Park, and Barnett Bank of Orlando, which Bank he also helped organize.

A past director of the Orlando Area Chamber of Commerce, Mr. Linton is also a past President of PESO. Indeed, without Criag Linton, there might never have been a PESO. Originated as a Symphony idea and project, under Linton's guidance, PESO was organized by three hard-working ladies; Jean Cooksey, Ardis Fratt, and Marilyn Wilson. Their unbelievable dedication and hard work resulted in the PESO we know today — providing badly-needed support to the area's cultural organizations on a continuing basis.

Mr. Linton, an avid tennis player, is a past Vice President of Florida Tennis Youth Foundation. He is also a past member of the President's Council of Rollins College, and is presently serving as President of both the Central Florida Development Committee and the Central Florida Tennis Confederation.

Craig Linton's interest in music began when he was a student in a Quaker Prep school in Philadelphia. He is extremely knowledgeable in musical matters, and possesses an extensive record collection. His interest in and support of the Florida Symphony is ongoing, and his talents as an organizer in the orchestra's behalf remain in demand.

106

George B. Gibson

GEORGE B. GIBSON - 1968-69 and 1969-70

Mr. George B. [Buzz] Gibson has been associated with pulp, paper and paperboard industries for virtually his entire business career, following his graduation from Northwestern University in 1921.

During his career, he has had wide experience in all phases of the paper industry, ranging from the invention of a new mechanical process of paper making to the officership of one of the large corporations of the paper industry—Union Bag & Paper Corporation—where he was Vice-President, General Sales Manager and Director of the company. He was also associated with International Paper Company and Container Corporation of America.

During World War II, he spent a great deal of time in Washington as a member of the War Production Board Pulp Allocation Committee of the paper industry, and he also served as Chairman of the Industries Advisory Committee of the O.P.A.

For over twenty years he has been Managing Director of the Fourdrinier Kraft Board Institute, an organization whose relationship to the paper industry parallels that of the Steel Institute to the steel industry.

A basic function of the Institute was that of research and the development of new markets. He successfully created the ideas and directed the conversion of the citrus industry, and many items of produce of the produce industry, from the use of wood boxes to paperboard boxes.

The most outstanding success that Mr. Gibson has had was in the development of the concept of a new method for the packaging, shipping, and merchandising of bananas that has revolutionized the entire banana industry.

This work was initiated in 1957 and still is in process of completion, but there is hardly a spot in the world today, whether it be the French Ivory Coast of Africa, to the Islands of the Caribbean, to the countries of Central America or South America—that is, wherever bananas are grown—that this new concept is not being employed.

Mr. Gibson first became a Director of the Florida Symphony in 1965. He became Vice-President of the Symphony in 1966, and served as Chairman of the Finance Committee in 1966 and 1967. He became President in 1968 and served for two years. During this same period of time, the Orchestra itself was increased in size and the season extended from 16 weeks to 20 weeks.

During the last year of his regime, $308,435 was raised for the Ford Foundation Matching Fund.

F. D. Streep, Jr.

F.D. STREEP, JR.-1970-71

F. D. Streep, Jr., is the owner of Streep Music Plaza and also the Streep Ticket Agency, which handles ticket reservations and sales for most of the musical, theatrical, and sports events appearing in Orlando, Winter Park, and even further afield. With his extensive background in both music and management, he was a 'natural' as President of the Florida Symphony Society, Inc.

Including 1970-71, when he served as President, he has been a member of the Society's Board of Directors for twelve years. His year as President was the fifth and final year of the Ford Foundation Matching Fund drive, and since this was the crucial hour - when the Fund had to be matched - it was a busy time of fund-raising. He, and - indeed - all the workers, were elated when a contribution of $100,000 arrived from the Edyth Bush Foundation, materially aiding the drive toward the magic half-million mark.

Though the orchestra carried a sizeable deficit into the 1970-71 season, it is to F.D. Streep, Jr.'s credit that this particular season ended up 'in the black', for the first time in many years.

Mr. Streep is a graduate of Missouri Military Academy, and attended the University of Kansas. He is a Navy veteran of World War II. A past president of the National Association of Music Merchants, he served on the Board of Directors of that organization for ten years. Mr. Streep has also been a Trustee of the American Music Conference, is a Past-president of the Central Florida Civic Music Association, and of the Orlando School Band Association.

Stephen T. Dean

STEPHEN T. DEAN - 1971-72, 1972-73

Stephen T. Dean, a member of the law firm of Carlton, Fields, Ward, Emmanuel, Smith & Cutler, P.A., of Orlando, Pensacola and Tampa, was elected to the Presidency of the Florida Symphony Society only weeks before the June 30, 1971 deadline for raising matching funds for the Ford Foundation half-million-dollar Grant.

It was a critical time, to say the very least, and there was no real certainty that the full matching half-million could be raised. In retrospect, Mr. Dean says: "With the help of everyone interested in the symphony, and particularly the staff and members of the Women's Committee, we qualified with contributions to spare! Considering our fears in June of that year, I think everyone was surprised, and no one more than I. There has never been, I think, such a community 'arising' before or since. When we went 'over the top', there was an exhiliration and excitement that fully justified all the work that was done."

Mr. Dean received his B.S. Degree in Economics from the Wharton School, University of Pennsylvania, in 1934, and his LL.B, J.S., in 1937 from the University of Pennsylvania.

He has professional memberships in the Florida, Pennsylvania, New York, American and Philadephia Bar Associations; American Bar Foundation; American Law Institute; Advisory Committee, New York University Tax Institute [to 1968] and University of Miami Estate Tax Institute; Chairman, Tax Committee of The Florida Bar [1966-67]; Chairman, Tax Committee of Orange County Bar Association [1970-71]; Consultant, American Law Institute, Federal Estate and Gift Tax Reform Program.

Mr. Dean is co-author of Prentice-Hall, Tax Ideas; J.K. Lasser's Lasser's Income and Estate Tax; and The Florida Bar CLE Will Drafting and Estate Planning Manual.

He has contributed articles to various law journals, and has been speaker at many tax institutes in the United States.

When he was practicing law in Philadelphia, his firm, of which he had been a member some twenty years, had represented the Philadelphia Orchestra since 1913, and all members of the firm enjoyed a special relationship with Mr. Eugene Ormandy, the conductor, and those responsible for the success of that outstanding orchestra. Related to that representation was also the representation of the Academy of Music, which housed the orchestra and many other cultural events. One of Mr. Dean's last jobs in Philadelphia, before coming to Orlando in 1959, was the reorganization of the Academy of Music.

112

Warren R. Winn, Jr.

WARREN R. WINN, JR. 1973-74

When Warren R. Winn, Jr. was elected to the Presidency of the Florida Symphony Society in 1973, past-president Stephen T. Dean succeeded to the post of Chairman of the Board. Internal organizers both, these two men vastly improved relations between the Board, volunteers, Arms of the Symphony, and orchestra members, themselves. Businessmen as well as adept organizers, Winn and Dean reorganized the Florida Symphony into a viable business organization, with improved flow of both communications and responsibility. The phenomenal growth of the orchestra demanded such action, and they were ideally suited to carry it out.

Warren R. Winn, Jr., is kept exceptionally busy as Regional Manager for Eastern Air Lines, but seems to find time for a variety of other interests.

Born in East Orange, N.J., he was educated at the U.S. Naval Academy [which may account for his avid interest in sailing, and the fact that he sails the "4 Winns" whenever possible], the University of Florida, and the University of Minnesota.

He has been active in civic affairs in Orlando, not only with the Florida Symphony Society, but as chairman of the Florida Citrus Invitational Golf Tournament, President of PESO, director of the Orlando Area Chamber of Commerce, Director and Vice-president of Central Florida Development Committee, Director of Mid-Florida Council of International Visitors, and Board member of Committee of 200, Orlando Chamber of Commerce. He was recipient of the 1966 President's Award from the Orlando Chamber.

Mr. Winn is a member of American Arbitration Association, St. Petersburg Yacht Club, U.S. Power Squadron, Beta Theta Pi, Navy Alumni, Board member Pan American Bank, Mystic Seaport Association, and Loch Haven Art Center, member and Director of the Citrus Club. He is also an active member of the citrus industry, and a citrus grower.

Mr. Winn is married to the former Phoebe Warner, of Orlando, and they are the parents of two grown daughters.

Hugh J. Jones, Jr.

HUGH J. JONES, JR. 1974-75

Hugh J. Jones, Jr., is—at 38—the youngest president the Florida Symphony Society has known in its quarter century of growth. Mr. Jones served as Treasurer of the Florida Symphony Society for four years prior to his elevation to the Presidency.

Mr. Jones is also a past president of one of the Arms of the Florida Symphony Society, Inc., the Associate Board. He is a member of the PESO Board, and in this last capacity, has been Chairman of the PESO TV Auction for the past three years.

Though born in Long Island, New York, Mr. Jones has lived for the past thirty-two years in Orlando, and attended public schools here. He is a graduate of the University of Florida, and a partner in the CPA firm of W. O. Daley & Co.

In a personal testimony to the benefit of Youth Concerts, Mr. Jones says that his interest in music and the Symphony actually began when he was a student at the old Concord Park Elementary School, and Yves Chardon—first conductor of the Florida Symphony Orchestra—presented a concert in the school's Spanish-type auditorium. The sound of the orchestra in that picturesque setting was so overwhelming that he has never forgotten it. His symphonic interest began at that moment, and has carried through to the present.

Mr. Jones is married to the former Barbara Hagan of Orlando, and they are the parents of three children.

THE ARMS
OF
THE FLORIDA SYMPHONY SOCIETY, INC.

The Women's Committee

The first Arm of the Florida Symphony Society, Inc., was the Women's Committee. However impressive the contributions of the other Arms have been, the Women's Committee has continued to be the most stalwart, dependable aid for the Symphony Society, in every undertaking—particularly fund-raising—along with its assigned responsibilities.

When the Women's Committee was formally organized in 1952, with Mrs. Loomis C. Leedy as its first president, it was just a small band of willing workers. When they had a membership luncheon or party, they brought their own food. They had no money at all! Every dollar they received was a triumph, and carefully hoarded to turn over to the Symphony. When they fanned out to help the Symphony raise money for that first small budget, they were wide-eyed, innocent, timid and SCARED. They soon got over that, for they all began to realize that they weren't asking for money for themselves, they were really acquainting the community with one of life's greatest gifts, the opportunity to hear fine music.

The Florida Symphony Society, Inc., had foreknowledge of the power of women on the march. In November, 1951, with one concert season behind it, and plans for the 1951-52 season made, Miss Helen Ryan and Miss Rose Phelps called Mrs. A. H. Smith, Jr., into the office and put the orchestra's monetary problem before her. As a consequence, she rallied some two hundred women of the Central Florida area to come to a meeting in the San Juan Hotel ballroom to plan a mammoth fund-raising drive. It was decided that they would try in one intensive week of hard work to raise the money needed.

This was not just an Orlando-Winter Park undertaking. Although women from these cities were certainly a part of it, other communities were also involved.

Chairmen for various divisions were Mrs. Julian Carter, Orlando, Mrs. Frederick Dunn-Rankin, Winter Park, Mrs. B. C. Stewart and Mrs. Frank Ross, Apopka, Mrs. R. M. Thoren, Gotha and Oakland, Mrs. Charles Ginn, Sanford, Mrs. Frank Chase, Windermere, Mrs. James Brock and Mrs. Bert Roper, Jr., Winter Garden, and Mrs. J.W. Shaw, Mount Dora.

Miss Helen Ryan was chairman for special gifts, Mrs. Arthur Frentz [the former Mrs. Richard Walker] was Headquarters chairman to receive reports, Jack Pedrick was chairman for business contributions [he was one of two men on the committee], and Mrs. George Newhart was chairman for the Campaign dinner.

Mrs. W. E. Botts, Harrison Hollander, and Mrs. A.H. Spivack were in charge of publicity. Miss Margaret Piper and Mrs. McCullough Maguire were chairmen of the Speakers' Bureau. Mrs. R. S. Hogue was chairman of the Young People's Concert Series, which, it was expected, would interest many parents.

It was a BUSY week, but a successful one. Officers and directors of the Florida Symphony Society decided that more important than the money raised was the new interest engendered in the Florida Symphony Orchestra by the contacts with so many people.

The Women's Committee has grown in membership and strength, and in its capacity to help the orchestra. Presidents of the Committee have been women of many talents, and each has inspired committee members to great accomplishment.

I call your attention to the list of all past Presidents of the Women's Committee, which is found in the Appendix. It is an Honor Roll, and a measure of the devotion of each and every President.

Recently, Marion Jennings [1965-66] invited all past Presidents who were in town to a luncheon at the Winter Park Raquet Club, and it was a happy gathering. They reminisced about funny things that happened in their time in office...

Twenty years or so ago, money was very scarce [does that sound like yesterday?] and when the great sum of $230 was raised, there was rejoicing. Now, the Women's Committee raises thousands of dollars each year.

One early POPS Concert, in January of 1962, was called "A Carnival of Music", and the Creative Arts Department of Rollins College created papier maché animals and other 'carnival' figures, which were hung from the ceiling in Municipal Auditorium. They placed tables on the floor of the Auditorium, and sold refreshments.

The luncheon guests talked about the crowded old Florida Symphony office in the San Juan Hotel, where Helen Mason, Colleen Pope, and Shirley Slaughter tried to get work done in all the confusion. Helen Mason said they'd have had more room working under her kitchen table. The place was so crowded that one year they had to stack the music for the opening concert on the floor all around the room. However, even if conditions weren't ideal, the price was certainly right. During his lifetime, Dr. A.H. Spivack donated the San Juan facilities for the use of the symphony. Lots of work was accomplished in those old offices, and many friendships were made there.

They spoke, with wonderment, of the fact that we got Van Cliburn here just after he had won the Tschaikovsky Competition. He has been back at least twice since, but that first appearance was something else! Folding chairs were set up on the stage to accomodate the overflow crowd, to the horror of the Fire Marshal, naturally. However, he relented and allowed this unprecedented situation, after extracting a promise from Symphony Management that such a thing would never, ever, be considered again.

There was the time that Mrs. Violet Dunham went to Mr. James E. Strates, whose Strates Shows were in winter quarters nearby, and borrowed the shows' trolley - a bright, attention-getting vehicle. A group rode in it all over town, blasting out: "A Dollar Today - A Symphony Tomorrow!"..."Give a Dollar".

The late Mrs. Dunham was a powerhouse in everything she attempted. She had been a successful business woman, but now, having reached an age when she might well forget work and enjoy herself, she was as full of steam as ever. It was Mrs. Dunham, in the early days of the symphony, who helped find lodging for the orchestra musicians as they arrived from the North to play here for the season. She met them, drove them around and saw that they were comfortably settled.

The Women's Committee sponsored progressive bridge parties, which were reasonably successful, at least for a time.

They talked of the big buttons they had for one campaign, with "Bach It To Me", in pop-art lettering and wild colors, printed on them.

There were the many beautiful Fashion Shows. When former "Miss America" Bess Myerson arrived to be fashion commentator for one show, the script that had been prepared for her was AWFUL. So Mary MacDonald, Marion Jennings and Corinne Duckworth sat up all night rewriting it. It read beautifully, and the 3,000 people who came to the show agreed that the event was a great success. There have been other celebrities here as fashion commentators — Anita Bryant, Eva Gabor,

120

and such luminaries, but the real stars are the women who work so hard to achieve this success.

They talked of the fashion show when Dot Ellis had all the priceless paintings on display for the edification of the guests and how nervous they all were, afraid something would happen to this art.

Some one brought up the time when the treasurer had a nervous breakdown, and the Committee has never found out what happened to the money they had banked up to that time.

Another time a well-dressed woman walked in and picked up a big armload of the beautiful Florida Heritage Cook Books which Joyce Vickers and Sheila Reich had compiled for the benefit of the Symphony. These books were a treasure in any kitchen, and worth much more than the $3.75 they were charging. Anyway, the woman left a check for $70, and it was no good — signer unknown!

The Women's Committee sponsored the premiere of the motion picture, "Johnny Tiger", starring Robert Taylor and Ursula Theiss, which was filmed nearby. When the stars arrived, the courtly Robert Taylor said: "Never before have I seen so many beautiful, and beautifully dressed women!" They knew it was a banal remark, but you should have HEARD him, they say. Guess it was just another one of those occasions when you had to BE there to appreciate it.

They talked about the gorgeous backdrop for one of their Fashion Shows, painted by Bob Singleton, then of Jordan-Marsh Display Department, now a serious and respected artist.

Mr. Irving Gibbs came in for compliments—he sponsored their first fashion show — and this owner of a downtown boutique, Gibbs-Louis Dress Shop, has always supported the Florida Symphony Orchestra.

They told of the time Dre [Mrs. Cloyde L.] Fausnaugh got twenty-eight parking tickets as she was hurrying around, gathering props for a show.

But it wasn't all bridge parties, fashion shows, and luncheons.

When Robert Anderson was President of the Symphony Society he told the Women's Committee what he wanted them to do: [1] to make money; [2] to increase their membership to 500. They were able to turn over to the Symphony Society $19,000 to $20,000 that year, and did increase their membership to 500.

The Florida Symphony Society, Inc., changed its by-laws and its administrative structure in July, 1971.

The Women's Committee was given specific responsibilities. It would be responsible for the Pops Concerts, the Florida Youth Symphony, and the Symphony Fashion Shows. They had been handling these activities anyway, as well as other special tasks they had volunteered to do from time to time, so it really didn't change their plans.

Mrs. Elwyn Evans, when she was Women's Committee President, had a most efficient way of finding the proper places for the members to accomplish the most. She had specific committees — an Auditorium Committee, Educational Committee [to help with the school concerts in the auditorium, and distribute tickets to the schools], Staff Assistant Committee [to help in the Symphony Office, when needed], Hospitality Committee, Membership Committee, Speaker's Bureau, Publicity, Transportation of Artists Committee. When there was anything to be done in any of those areas, she could immediately locate the members who could do it.

Among special contributions from members of the Women's Committee were the erudite and informative talks given by Betty [Mrs. Arnold J.] Wilson, Jr., called "Art of Listening" lectures, in Martin Hall, off the Rollins campus. Here the audience had a preview of the music they were to hear at the Symphony concerts, and a discussion of its meaning. Edna [Mrs. Walter B.] Johnston, another knowledge-able authority on music, was often a speaker for various clubs and groups.

A program to teach talented school students was started early in the existence of the Florida Symphony Orchestra. Musicians from the Orchestra would meet the students on Saturday mornings, and teach them how to play their chosen instruments. This was free, and many students came.

The Women's Committee was in charge of this program, and when the more serious students were ready to perform, they helped form a student orchestra. This Florida Youth Symphony, as it is now called, is presently a 65-member orchestra. It is conducted by Charles Gottschalk, who plays principal Trumpet with the Florida Symphony Orchestra. He also conducts many of the Florida Symphony Youth Concerts.

Members of the Florida Youth Symphony are recruited by announcements in the news media, and all are selected by audition.

Among Youth Symphony alumni now majoring in music at college are Ellen Arant, Anne Hendricks, Amanda Gertula, and Deborah Trigg, studying violin at Converse College. David Dillingham and Karl Bawel are studying violin at Florida State University. Nancy Crockford, Joleen Davis, Vicky Haan, and Tula Mihilas, are studying violin at Florida Technological University. Randy Weiss is studying violin at Oberlin College. Vicky Adkins is studying violin at Valencia Community College. John Price is studying bass at the University of Louisville, and Luan Fechter is studying clarinet at Peabody.

122

L to R: Dorian Koppenhaver, Alphonse Carlo, Charles Rex, Martha Straub, Priscilla Straub, Chris Rex, Holly Straub and Mrs. Alphonse [Katherine] Carlo — Youth Orchestra members in rehearsal circa: 1960.

Alumni of the Youth Orchestra who are now playing professionally are Violinists Dennis Cordell and Roger Penny, who have played with the Florida Symphony Orchestra, Chris and Charles Rex, who are playing with the Philadelphia Orchestra, and Cellist Barbara Smith, who played with the Summer Opera Festival Orchestra in Lake George, N. Y.

Other alumni of the Youth Orchestra include Sam Evans, tympanist, now with the U.S. Army Band; Howard van Heining, percussionist with the Baltimore Symphony; Kenneth Watts, trumpet, with the Air Force Band; and Larry Elam, who toured with the Juilliard Orchestra in Europe, and is now playing in a Symphony in the Orient.

Miss Eunice Randall, a member of the Women's Committee, was a great help in getting the Youth Orchestra started. Her father was a retired President of Travelers Insurance Company, and Miss Randall had traveled extensively and had seen many musical aggregations start and grow. She liked to work with young people, and was very faithful working on this project.

Seventeen scholarships were awarded to student musicians for 1974-75 by the Women's Committee of the Florida Symphony at a Florida Youth Orchestra Concert in November, 1974.

No wonder the Florida Symphony Society is proud of its Women's Committee.

The Associate Board

The respective memberships of the three Arms of the Florida Symphony Society, Inc., are often overlapping. The same people may belong to one, or two, or maybe all three of the Arms, although perhaps remain most active in one. It seems a satisfactory arrangement, and they can, in this way, avoid duplicating efforts and keep activities better coordinated. There has seldom been any sense of competition — everybody appreciates the fact that they are all working for the same cause— and each willingly cooperates, when it is needed.

In 1956, plans for a new Arm of the Symphony were made. A group of young adults, to be called an 'Associate Board,' became active, and adopted as their first project the sponsorship of the Symphony's Ballet Concerts.

The new Associate Board began the presentation of Children's Concerts, a good tie-in with the ballet. Conductor Henry Mazer had a way with children, and the very young set was soon learning about the instruments in the orchestra, and hearing good music. Programs were first called 'Lollipop Concerts'. As the Associate Board continued sponsorship, they became Children's Concerts, for kindergarten and elementary-age youngsters. Later, these concerts for the very young were titled "Pied Piper Concerts," and even later, "Magic of Music." Whatever their name, they have brought the joy of music to many young hearts.

The Associate Board also assumed the responsibility of sponsoring the annual Symphony Ball, and these have traditionally been imaginative and exceptionally beautiful social events. The Florida Symphony always plays for a short time to set the proper 'tone of elegance' for these Balls, and one of the many popular local dance bands plays for dancing for the remainder of the evening. Each of the Symphony Balls has had an interesting theme, which has been carried out in elaborate decorations. The Ball is a highlight of the social season each year. For many years, the Balls were held at the Country Club of Orlando, but other scenes have been chosen: once, a dazzingly-decorated Exposition Hall, and two memorable Balls have been held at the Contemporary Hotel at Walt Disney World.

124

Beginning in December, 1962, some especially excellent programs were presented on the Children's Concert Series. These included "Amahl and the Night Visitors", a children's opera; "Fun With Music", a program featuring the appearance, live, of Captain Kangaroo, and "Hansel and Gretel", a ballet program; all — naturally — with the Florida Symphony Orchestra. Other years, such ballets as "The Nutcracker," and the animated musical fantasy, "Babar, the Elephant" [both performed by the Ballet Royal] brought great entertainment to the children.

Although the Arms of the Symphony have always more or less stayed within certain activity bounds, in 1971, when the Florida Symphony Society changed its by-laws and administrative structure, the Associate Board was officially assigned two definite responsibilities: [1] It would be responsible for the Children's Concert Series, and [2] the annual Symphony Ball.

A few years ago, students at Park Maitland School, a private elementary school, gave such an excellent and well-received presentation of the play, "Oliver", that it was repeated, under Associate Board sponsorship, at Orlando's Municipal Auditorium, as part of the Children's Concert Series.

In the Appendix, all past Presidents of the various Arms are listed. Though space prohibits inclusion of committee chairmen and membership rolls, each person is remembered for every contribution he or she has made to promote the Florida Symphony Orchestra and the cause of good music in Florida.

You are not grains of sand on the beach. You, in our book, are a PIECE OF THE ROCK — the Rock of Remembrance, that is.

You have the heartfelt thanks of the entire community, and deserve them.

The Opera Gala Guild

How did Opera come to Orlando?

Back in 1957 Miss Helen Ryan, then, as now, imbued with the idea that Central Florida needed fine music in every form, went to a meeting of the Junior League of Orlando and suggested that since there was no opera here, perhaps the League might like to take Opera-in-Orlando as a project.

The idea appealed to them, and with their usual enthusiasm and efficiency they immediately started exploring the possibilities.

It was a big undertaking, they discovered, and would require an enormous amount of planning and work, but they concluded that it would be worth trying.

Opera was first presented in Orlando in 1958. It was called a "Gala Night of Opera", an evening of Opera-in-concert, sponsored by the Junior League of Orlando, Inc.

The League continued these operatic concerts — first adding costumes, then a bit of scenery — until 1963, when for the first time, they presented a fully-staged opera, with professional direction, sets, costumes and lighting. A Sunday matinee was added in 1966 — a very popular idea with older people who didn't want to drive at night.

As the task of producing a full opera grew, it became increasingly obvious to the League that the project should be turned over to the community where more manpower and resources could be found. An Opera Gala Guild was organized, with unlimited membership; and after three years orientation and guidance by the Junior League, who shared their experience with the new organization, the Opera Gala Guild of the Florida Symphony Society officially produced its first Opera in 1969. An affiliation with the Metropolitan Opera Guild followed the next year, and five more years of successful opera presentations have now become history.

Among the most-talked about things, along with the beautiful music, the opera stars who sang it and the Florida Symphony Orchestra who played for them, were the artistic programs of those

126

first years of Opera. They were the work of local artist, Robert Smith, whose professional name was Robert Curran. Big and handsome, they were great conversation pieces, and many an opera-goer carefully preserved these programs as a lasting memento of a beautiful musical experience.

The idea of opera didn't appeal to everybody. Some said it was too "High Brow". Others said: "Who wants to hear a bunch of loud-voiced singers hitting high notes in some foreign language we can't understand?" Some just didn't like anything about Opera. They said it was over-acted, you couldn't whistle the tunes — it was all overdone. And then there was the ribald comment: "Lots of people don't like Opera, but like W.C. Fields said about sex — it might not be good, but you have to admit, there's not anything else in the world like it!"

Happily, there were many, many people who were delighted that they could see Grand Opera right here, beautifully costumed, produced, and presenting the world's most celebrated Opera stars.

The Operas have to be chosen eighteen months in advance. Arrangements have to be made for professional set designer, costumer, lighting engineers, a volunteer chorus, and most important of all, the very best artists for the Opera's principal roles.

There is much going on back stage in a complicated operatic production. Members of the Opera Gala Guild, who work on all the details — gathering props, helping with decorations, etc. — soon catch the dedication and professional attitude of the real professionals they are working with, and it is a marvelous experience.

The Opera Gala Guild now has some 180 members. It is an open, no-limit membership which no doubt will grow, and there's something for everyone to do in the production of an Opera. If you doubt that statement just talk to anyone who was involved with the mammoth November, 1974 production of AIDA!

Funny things happen in all the busy confusion of production. During a rehersal of "La Boheme," the tenor [playing an artist starving in a garret] wasn't doing much acting — just walking through the part. Another character was supposed, at one point, to throw the starving artist some food — a fish from an onstage food stand. One of the Guild members had faithfully baked a dough 'fish' for each rehearsal, and wrapped it in a newspaper for the action. This night she and her husband decided to play a joke. Instead of the make-believe fish, they wrapped a real fish, slightly 'ripe,' and when the actor reached in the wrapper, pulled out his fish by the tail, and threw it — that really waked the tenor up! Fortunately, opera singers are known for playing jokes on each other, so he took it well. We understand, however, that he was not 'starving' enough to eat it!

A Grand Opera production is a costly undertaking, and the Opera Gala Guild discovered that the 1973-74 season's opera, "Daughter of the Regiment", was quite expensive. But "Daughter" was nothing to compare with the cost of the 1974-75 season's "Aida". The Gala Guild chose this grandest of operas to celebrate the orchestra's 25th anniversary season. It had a monstrous cast, and adjusting hems and fitting those lavish rented costumes was a big task.

The more elaborate the production, the higher the cost. "Aida," magnificent as it was, could not be afforded often.

Since the Guild is unwilling to lower its standards, it has had to look for various fund-raising projects to support first-class opera. Last season, the Guild sponsored a brand-new project — The Designers Show House.

Local interior designers took over the large mansion of the late Mrs. Grace Phillips Johnson, and each room — as well as the gardens — exhibited the newest in designer ideas. Hundreds of guests visited the place during the time it was on display, paying a nominal admission fee for the privilege. It was such a profitable venture that we may look forward to an annual Show House, at least in the forseeable future.

When the by-laws were written for the Opera Gala Guild, a two-fold purpose was stated: [1] To present Opera in Orlando, and [2] to support the Florida Symphony Orchestra. Opera lovers in Central Florida agree that the Junior League of Orlando for many years carried out this purpose, and the Opera Gala Guild has continued this great tradition.

Names of the presidents who have headed the Opera Gala Guild may be found in the Appendix.

THE FORD FOUNDATION
TRUST FUND GRANT

Robert T. Anderson was President of the Florida Symphony Society, and Helen Ryan Executive Vice President and General Manager, when they learned of the possibility of receiving a Grant from the Ford Foundation. They immediately saw the possibilities in being considered for participation in the Ford bounty. It was a time for serious thinking, and careful planning. When the Florida Symphony Orchestra was chosen as one of the sixty-one grantee orchestras across the nation, from more than two hundred applicants, it was evident that both Board and management had presented the cause of the orchestra well. The office rejoiced along with Mr. Anderson and Miss Ryan, for they, too, had participated in the meticulous job of presentation.

The Florida Symphony Orchestra's 'share' of the $80.2 million in total grants from the Ford Foundation was $600,000 — in two parts. $500,000 was in endowment funds, and this amount had to be matched by the community within a five-year period. $100,000 was in expendable funds, to be distributed at a rate of $20,000 per year, starting in 1967, until they were exhausted in 1971.

The Grant was not only subject to the condition that the Florida Symphony match Ford's half-million by June 30, 1971, but also the condition that the orchestra continue to raise its annual operating funds, as it had in the past.

The $500,000 raised locally was to be placed in a Trust, completely unencumbered, with only the income available to the orchestra until June 30, 1976. On this same date, the Ford Foundation was to release its grant of $500,000 to the orchestra.

This total of $1,000,000 in endowment funds was designed to ensure greater stability for the future growth and continued success of the symphony program. The earnings from both the Ford Grant and the Matching Fund would be available to help defray operational costs of the orchestra until the full million was received in 1976.

Obviously, this Grant to the Florida Symphony provided an opportunity of unprecedented magnitude. Initially, every dollar contributed locally to the Matching Fund became a potential $2.00 for the support of the orchestra. Also, receipt of the Ford Grant meant we

130

had attained national recognition, as a symphony orchestra of both ability and promise.

In making the Grant, the Ford Foundation publicly recognized the high professional standing of the Florida Symphony, and its potential for even greater excellence. This recognition of superior achievement has helped provide a new dimension of musical enrichment to the Central Florida community.

Talented musicians are now, and will continue to be attracted to the area to fill teaching positions in the schools, thus enriching the educational opportunities afforded to thousands continually.

Though the Florida Symphony received notice of its Ford Grant in June of 1966, it was not until 1969 that a major Matching Fund Drive was conducted. Frank Hubbard got the ball rolling. Mrs. John [Happy] Sterchi and 'Buzz' Gibson officially headed the drive, and hundreds of workers helped. In the hope that the full half-million could be 'wrapped up', a professional fund raiser was hired to lend his talents to the cause. Despite all this, the total on hand at the end of the drive was only $279,000.

In February, 1971, merely four months prior to the June 30, 1971 deadline for raising the matching $500,000, well over $200,000 was still needed!

The scramble to meet the deadline was a real cliff-hanger. Workers went out in all directions, tapping every source they knew. Many in the community who had never worked for the symphony before, joined in to help.

Every day was filled with excitement. Every report was greeted with cheers. On June 29, it was found that $41,036 was still needed. Workers manned 'pick up' runs virtually around the clock during those last few days, going physically to pick up donations from contributors in all areas of the county and from all walks of life.

On June 30, 1971 — the very last day — miracles happened. Over $60,000 literally poured in to push the Matching Fund well over the top. What a wonderful happening! The office was crowded with workers all talking at once, like the Stock Exchange on a wild day, answering telephones, assisting people coming into the office with everything from pennies to portfolios. It was not until shortly after 8 P.M. that evening that the announcement was made that the deadline had been met. Champagne corks popped, toasts were drunk, and an office full of giddy symphony workers held a celebration that had been five years in the making.

There were half a million reasons that the drive succeeded. Here are come of the major ones.

Walter Windsor, Manager of WFTV, Channel 9, put on an hours-long TV Marathon which brought the plight of the orchestra to

131

the public — and the public, in turn, responded dramatically.

Hugh and Jeanette McKean's own generous gift, and their contact with wealthy Ira Koger, of Jacksonville, for his large gift, helped materially.

An anonymous donor sent in a large gift in the last few hours, which was literally the 'put-over-the-top' gift.

But without the thousands of small contributors, the hundreds of man [and woman] hours spent on the project, and the absolute 'blitz' of publicity which all area News Media had provided, the impossible could never have been achieved. Not one gift can be minimized.

There are so many names that could be mentioned. Those who participated most actively in this last-ditch drive were F.D. Streep, Jr., Stephen T. Dean, Katie [Mrs. Paul] Hayne, Hugh Jones, Howard Gordon, Helen Ryan, Jim Barker, Betty Daniel and Suzie Boice.

Over 2,000 individuals and 200 business firms contributed to the $500,000 Matching Fund.

Both individuals and groups tried many clever ideas for money-raising. Lois Lawrence and Jim Barker gave a 'non-concert', complete with program listing of the people who would not perform, and requested $5.00 per couple from those who were invited not to attend. Some sent checks for considerably larger amounts, with the notation that they were 'not bringing' several other couples. The non-concert brought in several thousand dollars to the Ford Matching Fund — a better track record, profitwise, than some concerts which have been held!

Then there was the FORD 500 RACE, also Jim Barker's brainchild. Originally it was a sort of lottery-type project, but that raised all sorts of legal problems [they even got a ruling from the State's Attorney General, Robert Shevin] and the plan was adjusted to work like a pyramid. Ten women on the Key Committee each secured ten women more, and they in turn secured ten women each, and so on and on and on. Each person involved paid $1.00 and their name went into the pot to take a chance on prizes being offered. Obviously, hundreds upon hundreds were eventually involved. Each got a big yellow sticker emblazened with the Race theme, FORD 500. The big prize was — naturally — a brand new Ford automobile [or cash equivalent] with many lesser prizes adding excitement to the drawing.

Mrs. Grace Phillips Johnson, generous local philanthropist, had taken several tickets in the names of the people who worked for her. Her chauffer was the ecstatic holder of the winning ticket for the new Ford automobile. He decided to take the money instead, as he and his wife thought it would be best to put the money in a Savings Account for their daughter's education.

132

Matching the Ford was a staggering job — but the happy result proved that when people are confronted with a crisis, they are usually equal to it.

Now, nearing the end of the ten-year Trust period, the Florida Symphony looks to the future with confidence. When the million-dollar Trust becomes truly 'ours', it can be put to use earning other dollars. Left untouched, the principal will grow, and form the basis of future economic stability for the orchestra.

The Florida Symphony's many friends — including many new ones attracted during the Ford Matching Fund Drive — know that, in spite of the Ford monies, the years ahead will not have clear sailing all the way. But they wouldn't miss it for anything! It promises to be a most interesting trip!

Helen Ryan admires the prize rose garden of Dr. George Opdyke of Winter Park, one of the Symphony's earliest Angels, Circa. 1951-52.

ANGELS AND SOME LUMINOUS TERRESTRIAL SYMPHONY SUPPORTERS

Music is well said to be the speech of angels.

— *Carlyle*

ANGELS, BENEFACTORS, SPONSORS

Under each of the above categories in the list of contributors to the Maintenence Fund of the Florida Symphony Society, Inc., are organizations and names dear to our hearts. If space permitted, we'd like to write another whole book on the many ways they have helped the Symphony.

There are also the Patrons, Donors, Associates, and the Participating friends, whom we are always happy to count on for their support.

You will find these names in your Symphony programs — something pleasant to read during the concert intermissions.

Read them — recognize them! They are the big reasons why we have such a fine Symphony Orchestra and they are the bedrock of our cultural community, for you will see these same names backing almost every worthwhile endeavor.

Although we have chosen only a few whose special contributions were noteworthy in the growth of the Orchestra, we might well have chosen many, for the Florida Symphony Orchestra stands on a very broad base of community support.

MISS JOY HAWLEY

Who can forget the annual appearance of Joy Hawley, at the intermission of one of the Florida Symphony concerts, as she made her witty yet moving appeal for the continuing support of the Symphony?

Joy Hawley was born in Salt Lake City, Utah, but somewhere in there she must have kissed the Blarney Stone. She was very persuasive.

She attended Stout Institute, Rockford College, and Cornell University.

Widely traveled, she was nationally known as a writer of successful direct mail advertising campaigns. She was also known for the exceptional business letters she produced.

She won the Direct Mail Advertising Award in London for one of her campaigns, and she was in great demand as a speaker on advertising subjects.

Joy Hawley

Among her clients were the Atlantic Monthly, Metropolitan Museum, American Federation of Art, Link-Belt Company and others. Industrial firms and cultural organizations employed her to teach their executives how to write effective business letters.

Miss Hawley and Miss Helen Ryan bought the well-known Whistling Oyster Gift Shop and Tea Room in Ogunquit, Maine, and later established a Whistling Oyster gift shop in Orlando for the winter seasons.

From the beginning, Miss Hawley was vitally interested in helping the Florida Symphony Orchestra get established. Capitalizing on her wide acquaintance among industrialists in her former advertising career, and the monied clientele which patronized the Whistling Oyster, she contributed her great know-how with these people to raising money for the Orchestra.

Joy Hawley was known for her imaginative ideas, and her sense of humor. Her business partner, Helen Ryan, now says that Joy had to have a sense of humor to put up with Miss Ryan taking so much time from the business to work with the Symphony.

Joy Hawley was a charming hostess, and could always entertain her guests with a performance of her amazingly talkative parakeet, Presto. Presto usually stayed in his cage when guests were there, but once two men were standing near his cage and were startled when the bored Presto, not being included in their conversation, came our with "Peter Piper picked a peck of pickled peppers — that's hard to say. Can you do it?" They were so amused they didn't budge from his cage, and Presto obliged by going through his extensive repertoire.

Miss Hawley died in August, 1964, after a long illness. It was a sad day for the Symphony and for her many friends. She gave not only of her money, but of herself and her talents.

MRS. LEONARD DYER

Mrs. Jessica Hofstetter Dyer was one of the founders of the Florida Symphony Society. A former vice president and director of the Society, she was an ardent supporter of the Florida Symphony Orchestra and the former Symphony Orchestra of Central Florida.

Mrs. Dyer was also a founder of the Bach Music Festival Society and a supporter of Rollins College Music programs.

A native of Clinton, Iowa, she received her academic degree from Cornell College, Mt. Vernon, Iowa in 1904, and her degree in music from Oberlin Conservatory of Music in 1908.

After her graduation from the Conservatory, she taught piano and music history while holding the position of assistant dean of women at Cornell College until 1909.

138

From 1909-1913 Mrs. Dyer studied piano with Josef Lhevinne in Berlin, Germany. She taught piano at the Knox School in Tarrytown, N.Y., until 1919, when she established her own music studio in New York City, which she operated until her marriage to Leonard Huntress Dyer in 1927. Mrs. Dyer was listed in the New York Social Register.

The Dyers moved to Winter Park in 1933, and Mrs. Dyer was engrossed in the life of music she found here, until her death, at the age of 85, on December 26, 1971.

"She was the greatest inspiration we had," said Miss Helen E. Ryan, then general manager of the Florida Symphony Society, Inc., "and the greatest help. We could never measure her friendship. She was a modest, unassuming lady. She never wanted credit for anything. She was both a valued friend and a valued contributor, and she will be missed."

MISS MARY LENORE KNAPP

Miss Mary Knapp was a strong supporter of the Florida Symphony Orchestra for many years. Her interest included serving on the Board of Directors of the Florida Symphony Society, Inc., and in promoting

Mary Lenore Knapp

Symphony projects after she moved to Winter Park in 1950, with her father, the late Dr. Alfred A. Knapp, to become permanent residents instead of just winter visitors.

Miss Knapp was born in Brimfield, Illinois. She attended the public schools at Brimfield and earned distinction by winning gold and silver medals in the Peoria Declamatory contests. She attended private school in Vienna, Austria, then attended the Bradley Polytechnic Institute in Peoria through her second year of the college curriculum. Winning three scholarships, one from Bradley and two from the University of Chicago, she attended the University of Chicago for three years, receiving her AB Degree in 1918 and her Master's Degree in 1919, majoring in Latin.

Miss Knapp headed the Latin Department of the Princeton, Illinois Township High School for two years, then taught at Lyons Township at LaGrange, Illinois, for a year and at Bradley Institute for three and one-half years. She left Bradley to be employed as assistant to her late father, who was a distinguished physician, and had charge of his office in Peoria until his retirement.

While living in Illinois, Miss Knapp was a member of First Congregational Church of Peoria, Daughters of the American Revolution, American Branch of the Association of University Women, Society of Mayflower Descendants in the State of Illinois, Pilgrim John Howland Society, Alumni Association of Bradley Institute, Alumni Association of the University of Chicago, Women's Club of Peoria, Hispanic Institute of America and the Knapp Family Association of America. She held the office of Secretary of the Illinois State Federation of Music Clubs, and was Vice Presidnt [and acting President] of the Amateur Music Club of Peoria.

After moving to Winter Park, Miss Knapp continued to assist her late father and continued her very active interest in community affairs. She was a member of the Presbyterian Church of Winter Park, the Winter Park Women's Club, a life member of the Winter Park Garden Club and the East Circle, University of Chicago Alumni Association and the English Speaking Union.

Along with her very active membership in the Florida Symphony Society, Miss Knapp was also a member of the Audubon Society, a Patron of Rollins College, a member of the Visiting Nurses Association, the Loch Haven Art Center and the Florida Museum.

The Symphony Orchestra lost a good friend when Miss Knapp died, and she will be greatly missed. In her Will she remembered the Florida Symphony Orchestra most generously, so her work and support will continue.

140

DR. MARY L. LEONARD

The story of Dr. Mary L. Leonard is told in the "Forerunners of the Florida Symphony" section of this book, but it bears repeating.

She was, indeed, an angel, and the Symphony owes much to her efforts to keep symphonic music alive in this area. Working under difficulties, as she was, during the Depression, she did a remarkable job in bringing great music to the community for a number of years. She encouraged the participation of musicians who had had to leave their music careers, in order to make a living. She planned fine programs, and through her own love of music, and sense of responsibility, she was determined that this music should be heard.

A bequest, in her Will, to the Symphony which she loved, was a welcome aid to reactivating the Orchestra when it was again started, with no assets at all, except a willingness to try.

Dr. Mary Leonard will be remembered for her example, her practical gift to the Orchestra, and the joy which she brought to concert goers of that earlier day.

MISS ROSE PHELPS

One of the Florida Symphony Orchestra's best remembered "angels" was Miss Rose Phelps.

For many years Miss Phelps had come to Orlando with her distinguished father, Captain John Phelps — in fact, we didn't think the winter season had actually started until Captain Phelps' arrival.

Rose Phelps lived a great deal of her early life abroad, and had many friends all over the world. A graduate of Wellesley College, she had a life-long interest in music and cultural affairs. When she was in this country, she lived with her parents at their home, "Red Towers" in Teaneck, N.J., or at another of their homes in Hackensack, N.J., or their apartment in New York City. She was very active in the Church of the Ascension, on Fifth Avenue, New York, and had many philanthropic interests in this country and Europe as well as the Middle East, particularly Beirut.

Miss Phelps was by nature shy, but her sunny disposition and her many intersts kept her in touch with many people. She was selfless and charitable — a person who loved people regardless of race, color or creed.

In whatever Rose Phelps was interested, she gave her all, and never spared herself. When she became interested in the Florida Symphony Orchestra, she served on the Board of the Symphony Society, she worked in the office, and she toured with the Orchestra.

Rose Phelps

Whenever money was needed, and it was always needed, of course, it was Rose Phelps who came to the rescue, and she used her considerable means to help in many ways.

After her father's death she decided to make her home in Orlando and she devoted the last years of her life to the Florida Symphony Orchestra.

She had an apartment in the home of her good friend, Norah [Mrs. E. Harold] Johnson, and seemed very happy to be here, doing the work she loved. On a visit to friends in Miami in October, 1952, Miss Phelps suffered a fatal heart attack. Her great personal inspiration and financial support had been invaluable in the early growth of the Symphony. She came as close as anyone could to being indispensable. In her will she left $50,000 to the Florida Symphony Orchestra to help continue the work she had begun.

MISS MARGARET PIPER

Miss Margaret Piper, who served many years as a member of the Board of Directors of the Florida Symphony Society, and supported the cause of the Florida Symphony Orchestra in many ways, was indeed a force for music, art and literature in this area.

She and her sister, Miss Warrene Piper, and their mother, were winter vistors for years before the Misses Piper decided to make their home here after their mother's death. They bought a home at 1120 Palmer Avenue, Winter Park, where they entertained often, and their garden was a show place.

Miss Piper was born in Montclair, N.J., but she was educated in Australia where the family moved when her father's business interests took him there. The family took occasional trips to Europe and America, and then lived in New York City for four years, dividing their time between Florida, New York and New England, with trips to Europe and France until 1941.

Margaret Piper

The Misses Piper had English governesses and instructors at home while they lived in Australia, and not only did they acquire a superior education, with wide-ranging knowledge on many subjects, but they spoke with charming English accents. Since they were wise and witty and articulate, they were both in great demand as public speakers.

Miss Margaret Piper gave excellent book programs for many organizations in the area. But her interests did not stop with books, or the great collection of records of fine music which she enjoyed.

She was vitally interested in the community and the state, serving on the boards of Sorosis, the Orange County Chapter of American Red Cross, Young Women's Community Club, Community Chest, and the Central Florida Branch of the English-Speaking Union.

She was past president of the Winter Park-Orlando League of Women Voters, and was also State President of the Florida League of Women Voters. She served on the Executive Committee of the Citizens' Constitution Committee which worked for the revision of the State Constitution.

Miss Piper was a member of the Board of Governors of Orange Memorial Hospital, the boards of the Orlando Humane Society and the Orlando Art Association. She was also a member of the Friends of the Library of both Winter Park and Orlando, the Country Club of Orlando, and, in England, the Royal Society for the Prevention of Cruelty to Animals, the Royal Horticultural Society, Friends of Tewksbury Abbey, and the National Trust.

Her interest in animals was real. She always had two or three beautiful, well-trained but very pampered cats.

After her sister Warrene's death, Margaret Piper continued her travels, and her many activities, until her death in October, 1970.

MRS. EDYTH BUSH

There is sweet music here that softer falls
Than petals from blown roses on the grass.

— *Alfred Lord Tennyson*

The late Edyth Bush was a philanthropist in the grand tradition. Widow of multimillionaire industrialist, Archibald Granville Bush [of the Minnesota Mining and Manufacturing Company] she had shared his great interest in worthy institutions. After his death, Mrs. Bush continued her husband's benefactions, making substantial contributions to Rollins College, the Central Florida Civic Theater Building Fund [indeed, that theater was named the Edyth Bush Theater, in her memory], as well as to the Florida Symphony Orchestra.

144

Mrs. Bush maintained a great interest in all the performing arts throughout her life. Not only was she an actress and author, she was an accomplished pianist and composer. In 1966, both Mr. and Mrs. Bush were awarded honorary doctorate degrees from Rollins College in Winter Park. At that time, Mrs. Bush was praised as "a true humanitarian, a woman of courage and one devoted to goodness and beauty."

Mrs. Bush's death in November, 1972, was a great loss to the cultural community of Central Florida. However her devotion to beauty, and to the best of the arts, continues under the guidance of the Edyth Bush Charitable Foundation, Inc. The Florida Symphony is proud to express its gratitude to both Mrs. Bush and the Foundation for their continuing faith and support through many years.

APPENDIX

SEASON: 1950-51   CONDUCTOR: Yves Chardon

OFFICERS & MEMBERS OF EXECUTIVE COMMITTEE:

ROBERT S. CARR .... President
DR. A. H. SPIVACK .... Vice-President
MRS. RICHARD WALKER .... Secretary
JULIAN H. CARTER .... Treasurer

Dr. Clarence Bernstein	Roy H. Gibbs
George Bradshaw	Rose Phelps
Dr. Richard Chace	Ed Ray
Mrs. Leonard Dyer	Helen Ryan
Mrs. Henry J. Forman	C. L. Stanford
Homer Gard	John Tiedtke

Shirley Slaughter, Executive Secretary
Public Relations: Dr. K. R. Steady—Stewart Martin

BUDGET: $30,000 LENGTH OF SEASON: 8 Weeks # MUSCIANS: 40+

SUBSCRIPTION SERIES CONCERT DATES & PROGRAMS:

Preview Concert: March 23, 1950
Conductor: *Yves Chardon*

Program: *Saint-Saens*	Prelude to the Deluge
Bizet	L'Arlesienne Suite No. 1
	(Prelude and Adagietto)
Strauss	Tales of the Vienna Woods
Brahms	Symphony No. 1 (I and IV)
Sibelius	Finlandia

FIRST SEASON 1950-51

January 5, 1951

Weber	Euryanthe Overture
Beethoven	Symphony No. 5
Piston	Concerto for Orchestra
Rimsky-Korsakov	Capriccio Espagnol

January 26, 1951
Jesse Baker, Helen Moore, and Manly Duckworth, *Pianists*

Wagner	Die Meistersinger Prelude
Bach	Concerto for Three Pianos in C
Brahms	Symphony No. 3

146

February 8, 1951
Nenita Escandon, *Pianist*

Mozart	Magic Flute Overture
Beethoven	Concerto No. 5
Franck	Symphony in D Minor

February 22 and 23, 1951

Couperin-Milhaud	Overture and Allegro
Mozart	Symphony No. 40
Bizet	Children's Games Suite
Mendelssohn	Nocturne from "Midsummer Night's Dream"
Strauss	Suite from "Der Rosenkavalier"

March 9, 1951
Henriette de Constant, *Cellist*

Vivaldi	Primavera
Saint-Saens	Cello Concerto
Tchaikovsky	Symphony No. 5

March 24, 1951
Marilyn Cotlow, *Soprano;* William Carlton, *Baritone;* Central Florida Choral Society; text read by Howard Bailey before each number.

Brahms	German Requiem

SEASON: 1951-52   CONDUCTOR: Yves Chardon

OFFICERS & MEMBERS OF EXECUTIVE COMMITTEE:

JUDGE JOHN G. BAKER .... President
MISS ROSE PHELPS .... Executive Vice-President
DR. A. H. SPIVACK .... Vice-President
MRS. RICHARD H. WALKER .... Secretary
MR. JULIAN H. CARTER .... Treasurer

Mrs. John G. Baker	Mr. Roy H. Gibbs
Dr. Clarence Bernstein	Mrs. R. S. Hogue
Mr. George Bradshaw	Mr. Harrison Hollander
Dr. Richard Chace	Mrs. Walter B. Johnston
Mrs. Leonard Dyer	Miss Helen Ryan
Mrs. Henry J. Forman	Mr. John Tiedtke
Mr. Homer Gard	

Miss Shirley Slaughter, Executive Secretary
Mr. Robert Hoffman, Field Representative

BUDGET: $85,065   LENGTH OF SEASON: 12 Weeks   #MUSICIANS: 65

SECOND SEASON 1951-52

January 10, 1952

Bach	Mitropoulos, Fantasy and Fugue

Beethoven	Symphony No. 3
Copland	Quiet City
De Falla	Suite from Three-Cornerd Hat

January 23, 1952
Artur Rubinstein, *Pianist*

Mozart	Marriage of Figaro Overture
Chausson	Symphony in B Flat
Beethoven	Concerto No. 5

February 8, 1952
Jan Peerce,*Tenor*

Bach	Chorale Prelude: "O Man, Bewail Thy Grievous Sin"
Handel	No, of Dio
Mozart	Il Mio Tesoro from "Don Giovanni"
Debussy	Two Nocturnes, Nuages, Fetes
Verdi	Di Miei Bollenti Spiriti from "La Traviata"
Puccini	E Lucevan le stelle from "Tosca"
Dvorak	Symphony No. 5

February 22, and 23, 1952
Ruth Posselt, *Violinist*; Henriette de Constant, *Cellist*

Kabalevsky	Colas Breugnon Overture
Brahms	Double Concerto
Schumann	Symphony No. 3

March 14, 1952
Isaac Stern, *Violinist*

Prokofiev	Classical Symphony
Mendelssohn	Violin Concerto
Brahms	Symphony No. 2

March 28, 1952

Beethoven	Egmont Overture
Debussy	Prelude to Afternoon of a Faun
Strauss, Richard	Der Rosenkavalier Suite
Tchaikovsky	Symphony No. 4

SEASON: 1952-53   CONDUCTOR: Yves Chardon

OFFICERS & MEMBERS OF EXECUTIVE COMMITTEE:

JUDGE JOHN G. BAKER .... President
MRS. LEONARD DYER .... Vice President
DR. A. H. SPIVACK .... Secretary
MR. R. C. PRIBBLE .... Treasurer

Mr. William H. Bell	Mr. Harrison Hollander
Dr. Clarence Bernstein	Mrs. Walter B. Johnston

Mr. Robert S. Carr	Mrs. Loomis C. Leedy
Mr. Julian H. Carter	Mr. James A. Pittman
Dr. Richard Chace	Miss Helen Ryan
Mrs. Sherwood Foley	Mr. John Tiedtke
Miss Joy Hawley	Mrs. Richard H. Walker

David Simonds, Business Manager

BUDGET: $101,545 LENGTH OF SEASON: 10½ Weeks # MUSICIANS: 66

PRESIDENT OF WOMEN'S COMMITTEE: ..... Mrs. Loomis C. Leedy
Special Notes; Women's Committee Organized this season.

* * * * * * * * * *

Name of orchestra officially changed from 'Central Florida Symphony Orchestra' to 'Florida Symphony Orchestra'.

* * * * * * * * * *

Orchestra became fully-contracted (all-professional) this season.

THIRD SEASON 1952-53

January 9, 1953

Weber	Oberon Overture
Brahms	Haydn Variations
Khachaturian	Gayne Ballet Suite (3 Dances)
Sibelius	Symphony No. 2

January 22, 1953
Maurice Wilk, *Violinist*

Hindemith	Konzertmusik for Strings & Brass
Chausson	Poeme for Violin
Ravel	Tzigane
Mendelssohn	Symphony No. 5

February 6, 1953
William Masselos, *Pianist*

Roussel	Suite in F
Chopin	Concerto No. 2
Dukas	Sorcerer's Apprentice
Schubert	Rosamunde Ballet Music
Ravel	Bolero

February 16, 1953
Henriette de Constant, *Cellist*

Tcherepnin	Romantic Overture
Wagner	Siegfried Idyll
Beethoven	Symphony No. 8
Bloch	Schelomo
Borodin	Polovetzian Dances from Prince Igor

149

March 5, 1953
Monique de la Bruchollerie, *Pianist*

Schuman, William	Circus Overture
Moussorgsky	Pictures at an Exhibition
Tchaikovsky	Concerto No. 1

March 19, 1953
Bidu Sayao, *Soprano*

Bach-Mitropoulos	Fantasy and Fugue in D Minor
Schubert	Symphony No. 8
Mozart	Deh vieni, non tarder *and* Non so piu from "Marriage of Figaro"
Obradors, Fernando	Coplas do Curro dulce *and* Dos Cantares Populares
Sandoval, Miguel	El Marcao de las Esclavas
Braja, Ernani	Engenho Novo
Villa-Lobos	Bachianas Brasileiras No. 5
Longas, Federico	Piropo
Debussy	La Mer

SEASON: 1953-54   CONDUCTOR: Yves Chardon

OFFICERS & MEMBERS OF EXECUTIVE COMMITTEE:

MISS HELEN RYAN .... President
DR. A. H. SPIVACK .... Executive Vice President
MRS. LEONARD DYER .... Vice President
MR. ROY GIBBS .... Secretary
MR. R. C. PRIBBLE .... Treasurer

Mrs. George Baker	Miss Joy Hawley
Judge John G. Baker	Mr. Harrison Hollander
Mr. William H. Bell	Mrs. Walter B. Johnston
Dr. Clarence Bernstein	Mrs. Loomis C. Leedy
Mr. Robert S. Carr	Mr. J. W. Randall
Dr. Richard Chace	Mr. Frederick W. Sleight
Mrs. Elwyn Evans	Mr. John Tiedtke

Robert Craig, Business Manager

BUDGET: $104,533   LENGTH OF SEASON: 11 Weeks #MUSICIANS: 57

President of Women's Committee — Mrs. Loomis C. Leedy

FOURTH SEASON 1953-54

January 14, 1954

Dvorak	Carnival Overture
Moussorgsky	Prelude to Khovanstchino
Saint-Saens	Danse Macabre
Beethoven	Symphony No. 6

January 29, 1954
Edward Preodor, *Violinist*

Rossini	Barber of Seville Overture
Mendelssohn	Violin Concerto
Schubert	Symphony No. 9
Milhaud	Le Boeuf Sur Le Toit (Ox on the Roof)
	(listed as encore)

February 12, 1954
Monique de la Bruchollerie, *Pianist*

Massenet	Phedre Overture
Mozart	Symphony No. 41
Brahms	Concerto No. 2
Satie	Gymnopedies No. 1 and 2
Copland	John Henry
	(Satie and Copland listed as encore)

February 25, 1954
Edith Anthony and Thomas Benton, *Flutists*

Beethoven	Leonore Overture No. 3
Delius	Walk to Paradise Garden
Vivaldi	Concerto for Two Flutes
Mozart	Adagio for Flute (Anthony)
Schumann	Symphony No. 4
Barber	Adagio for Strings
Copland	John Henry
	(Barber and Copland listed as encore)

March 12, 1954

Brahms	Academic Festival Overture
Barraud, Henry	Offrande a une ombre
Schuman, William	Symphony for Strings
Mendelssohn	Symphony No. 5

March 26, 1954
William Primrose, *Violist*

Weber	Overture Der Freischutz
Barbirolli	Concerto on Handel Themes for Viola
Rubbra, Edmund	Concerto in A for Viola
Brahms	Symphony No. 4

SEASON: 1954-55   CONDUCTOR: Frank Miller

OFFICERS & MEMBERS OF EXECUTIVE COMMITTEE

MISS HELEN RYAN .... President
DR. A. H. SPIVACK .... Executive Vice President

FIFTH SEASON 1954-55

January 7, 1955

Wagner	Flying Dutchman Overture
Mendelssohn	Symphony No. 3
Moussorgsky	Night on Bald Mountain
Ravel	Le Tombeau de Couperin
Rimsky-Korsakov	Capriccio Espagnol

January 20, 1955
Sondra Bianca, *Pianist*

Glinka	Russlan and Ludmilla Overture
Handel	Water Music Suite
Andre-Bloch	Concerto-Ballet for Piano
Liszt	Concerto No. 1 in Eb
Enesco	Roumanian Rhapsody No. 1

February 4, 1955
Leonard Rose, *Cellist*

Beethoven	Coriolan Overture
Dvorak	Cello Concerto
Franck	Symphony in D Minor

February 17, 18, 19, 1955
(Concerts held in Winter Park High School Auditorium)

Wolfe-Ferrari	Secret of Suzanne Overture
Borodin	Symphony No. 2
Dukas	Sorcerer's Apprentice
Saint-Saens	Omphale's Spinning Wheel
Debussy	Iberia (No. 2 of Images)

March 3, 1955
Tossy Spivakovsky, *Violinist*

Weber	Euryanthe Overture
Beethoven	Symphony No. 7
Brahms	Violin Concerto

March 17, 1955
Dorothy Eustis, *Pianist*

Smetana	Bartered Bride Overture

Rachmaninoff	Concerto No. 2
de Falla	Three Dances from "The Three-Cornered Hat"
Strauss	Till Eulenspiegel

SEASON: 1955-56   CONDUCTOR: Frank Miller

OFFICERS & MEMBERS OF EXECUTIVE COMMITTEE

MISS HELEN RYAN .... President
DR. A. H. SPIVACK .... Executive Vice President
MRS. LEONARD DYER .... Vice President
MR. ROY GIBBS .... Secretary
MR. R. C. PRIBBLE .... Treasurer

Judge John G. Baker	Mr. Harrison Hollander
Dr. Richard Chace	Mrs. Walter B. Johnston
Mrs. Stanley Cleveland	Mr. John Masek
Mrs. Elwyn Evans	Mr. Ralph Meitin
Mrs. John Freeman	Miss Margaret Piper
Mr. Stephen Gregor	Mr. James Pittman
Miss Joy Hawley	Mr. Frederick W. Sleight
	Mr. John Tiedtke

David L. Cotton, Business Manager

BUDGET: $102, 834 LENGTH OF SEASON: 11 Weeks # MUSICIANS: 55

PRESIDENT OF WOMEN'S COMMITTEE: Miss Margaret Piper

SIXTH SEASON 1955-56

January 7, 1956
Ruth Hall, *Contralto*

Brahms	Symphony No. 1
Ibert	Divertissement
Verdi	La Forza del Destino Overture
de Falla	El Amor Brujo

January 21, 1956
Alice Anderson, *Soprano;* Ruth Hall, *Contralto;* Lamar Simmons, *Tenor;* Ross Rosazza, *Baritone;* Bach Festival Choir

Mozart	Marriage of Figaro Overture
Mozart	Symphony No. 40
Mozart	Requiem

February 4, 1956
Leonard Rose, *Cellist*

Berlioz	Roman Carnival Overture
Saint-Saens	Cello Concerto
Tchaikovsky	Variations on Rococo Theme
Sibelius	Symphony No. 1

February 13, 1956
Jorge Bolet, *Pianist*

| Mendelssohn | Ruy Blas Overture |

Prokofiev	Concerto No. 2
Beethoven	Symphony No. 1
Stravinsky	Firebird Suite

March 3, 1956
Alexander Schneider, *Violinist*

Rossini	Semiramide Overture
Mozart	Violin Concerto in A, K. 219
Copland	El Salon Mexico
Beethoven	Violin Concerto

March 17, 1956
Rudolf Firkusny, *Pianist*

Creston	Dance Overture
Rachmaninoff	Rhapsody on a Theme of Paganini
Ravel	Rapsodie Espagnole
Elgar	Enigma Variations

SEASON: 1956-57   CONDUCTOR: Frank Miller

OFFICERS & MEMBERS OF EXECUTIVE COMMITTEE

MISS HELEN RYAN .... President
DR. A. H. SPIVACK .... Executive Vice President
MRS. LEONARD DYER .... Vice President
MR. ROY GIBBS .... Secretary
MR. R. C. PRIBBLE .... Treasurer

Judge John G. Baker	Miss Mary Knapp
Mrs. Stanley Cleveland	Mr. John Masek
Mrs. Elwyn Evans	Mr. Julian Pace
Mrs. John Freeman	Miss Margaret Piper
Mr. Stephen Gregor	Mr. James Pittman
Mr. Harrison Hollander	Mrs. J. Hilbert Sapp
Mrs. Walter B. Johnston	Mr. Frederick W. Sleight
	Mr. John Tiedtke

David L. Cotton, Business Manager

BUDGET: $112,094   LENGTH OF SEASON: 12 Weeks # MUSICIANS: 55

PRESIDENT OF WOMEN'S COMMITTEE: Miss Margaret Piper

SEVENTH SEASON 1956-57

January 5, 1957

Rossini	La Gazza Ladra Overture
Schumann	Symphony No. 2
Rimsky-Korsakov	Scheherazade

January 12, 1957
Jerome Hines, *Bass*

Mozart	Magic Flute Overture
Chausson	Symphony in Bb
Mozart	Non piu andrai from "Marriage of Figaro"

Verdi	Ella giammai n'amo from "Don Carlo"
Gounod	Mefistofeles Serenade from "Faust"
Schumann	The Two Grenadiers
Traditional	Song of the Volga Boatman
Moussorgsky	Song of the Flea

January 17, 1957
Saul Eichner, *Clarinetist*

Haydn	Symphony No. 82 (L'ours)
Dello Joio	Clarinet Concertante
Franck	Le Chasseur Maudit, Symphonic Poem
Glinka	Kamarinskaja
Miklos Rozza	Theme, Variations, and Finale

February 2, 1957
Zadel Skolovsky, *Pianist*

Berlioz	Benvenuto Cellini Overture
Bizet	Symphony in C
Saint-Saens	Concerto No. 2
Milhaud	Suite Francaise

February 15 and 16, 1957
Alphonse Carlo, *Violinist*

Beethoven	Leonore Overture No. 2
Bruch	Violin Concerto No. 1
Griffes	White Peacock
Griffes	Pleasure Dome of Kubla Khan
Dohnanyi	Suite for Orchestra in F Minor

March 2, 1957
Dorothy Warenskjold, *Soprano*

Schubert	Symphony No. 5
Mozart	Deh Vieni, non tarder; Non so piu; and Dove sono from the "Marriage of Figaro"
Leoncavallo	Ballatella from "Pagliacci"
Puccini	Signore, ascolta; Tucche di gel from "Turandot"
Gounod	Il etait un roi de Thule; Je ris de me voir se belle from "Faust"
Kodaly	Hary Janos Suite

March 16, 1957
Jorge Bolet, *Pianist*

Gretry	Suite from Cephales et Procris
Dvorak	Symphony No. 4
Brahms	Concerto No. 2

March 23, 1957

Bloch	Concerto Grosso No. 1

Berlioz	Scherzo, Queen Mab, from "Romeo & Juliet"
Berlioz	Three Excerpts from "Damnation of Faust"
Strauss	Don Juan
Tchaikovsky	Francesca da Rimini

SEASON: 1957-58   CONDUCTOR: Frank Miller

OFFICERS & MEMBERS OF EXECUTIVE COMMITTEE:

MISS HELEN RYAN .... President
MRS. WALTER B. JOHNSTON .... Assistant to the President
DR. A. H. SPIVACK .... Executive Vice President
MRS. LEONARD DYER .... Vice President
MR. HERSHELL G. STUART .... Secretary
MR. GEORGE BAER .... Treasurer

Judge John G. Baker	Mr. Harrison Hollander
Mrs. F. Page Bussells	Miss Mary Knapp
Mrs. Stanley Cleveland	Mr. John Masek
Mrs. Elwyn Evans	Mr. Julian Pace
Mrs. John Freeman	Miss Margaret Piper
Mr. Stephen Gregor	Mrs. Harold E. Rose
Miss Joy Hawley	Mr. Frederick W. Sleight
	Mr. John Tiedtke

David L. Cotton, Manager
Miss Shirley Slaughter, Ticket Manager

BUDGET: $121,801 LENGTH OF SEASON: 12 Weeks # MUSICIANS: 64

PRESIDENT OF WOMEN'S COMMITTEE: Mrs. Roland Schacht

EIGHTH SEASON 1957-58

January 2, 1958

Tchaikovsky	Symphony No. 4
Debussy	Petite Suite
Dvorak	Scherzo Capriccioso
Wagner	Tannhauser Overture

January 9, 1958
Earl Wild, *Pianist*

Schubert	Symphony No. 7
Gershwin	Concerto in F
Gershwin	Rhapsody in Blue

January 16, 1958
Alphonse Carlo, *Violinist;* Otto Silverstein, *Violinist*

Bach	Concerto in D Minor for Two Violins
Beethoven	Symphony No. 4
Copland	Outdoor Overture
Mabel Daniels	Deep Forest
Frank Miller	Procession
Don Gillis	Symphony No. 5½

156

January 23, 1958
George London, *Baritone*

Haydn	Symphony No. 101 (Clock)
Mozart	Mademina; Finch 'Han del vino from "Don Giovanni"
Verdi	E sogno? O realta? from "Falstaff"
Loeffler, Charles Martin	Memoirs of My Childhood
Wagner	O du, mein holder abendstern from "Tannhauser"
Wagner	Wotan's Farewell and Magic Flower Music from "Die Walkure"

February 6, 1958
Rudolf Firkusny, *Pianist*

Hanson	Symphony No. 1
Alfven, Hugo	Midsommarvaka
Grieg	Concerto in A Minor
Sibelius	Finlandia

February 27, 1958
Alphonse Carlo, *Violinist;* Geraldine Gee, *Violist*

Mozart	Symphony No. 35
Mozart	Sinfonia Concertante in Eb, K. 364
Lalo	Symphonie Espagnole
Strauss	Emperor Waltz

March 13, 1958
Jesse Baker, *Pianist*

Schubert	Rosamunde Overture
Rimsky-Korsakov	Intro. and Proc. from Coq d'Or
Rimsky-Korsakov	Concerto No. 2
Mendelssohn	Overture, Scherzo, Nocture, and Wedding March from "Midsummer Night's Dream"
Chabrier	Espana Rhapsody

March 20, 1958
Eileen Farrell, *Soprano*

Humperdinck	Hansel and Gretel Overture
Prokofiev	Classical Symphony
Puccini	Vissi d'arte from "Tosca"
Mascagni	Voi lo sapete from "Cavalleria Rusticana"
Verdi	Ernani involami from "Ernani"
Wagner	Dich theure halle from "Tannhauser"
Weber	Ocean Thou Mighty Monster
R. Strauss	Seven Veils
Wagner	Meists'r Preld

SEASON: 1958-59   CONDUCTOR: Frank Miller

OFFICERS & MEMBERS OF EXECUTIVE COMMITTEE

MISS HELEN RYAN .... President
MRS. WALTER B. JOHNSTON .... Assistant to the President
DR. A. H. SPIVACK .... Executive Vice President
MRS. LEONARD DYER .... Vice President
MR. HERSHELL G. STUART .... Secretary
MR. GEORGE BAER .... Treasurer

Judge John G. Baker   Mr. John Masek
Mrs. F. Page Bussells   Mrs. Harley Morse
Mrs. Elwyn Evans   Mr. Julian Pace
Miss Joy Hawley   Miss Margaret Piper
Mr. Harrison Hollander   Mrs. R. L. Schacht
Mrs. R. D. Keene   Mr. Frederick W. Sleight
Mrs. Loomis C. Leedy   Mr. Raymond Stevens
                             Mr. John Tiedtke

David L. Cotton, Manager
Miss Shirley Slaughter, Ticket Manager

BUDGET: $135,263 LENGTH OF SEASON: 12 Weeks # MUSICIANS: 63

PRESIDENT OF WOMEN'S COMMITTEE: Mrs. Roland Schacht

NINTH SEASON 1958-59

January 2, 1959
Wagner   Rienzi Overture
Rachmaninoff   Symphony No. 2
Turnia   Danzas Fantasticas
Debussy   Prelude to afternoon of a Faun
Tchaikovsky   Romeo and Juliet

January 8, 1959
Igor Gorin, Baritone

Haydn   Symphony No. 88
Giordano   Nemico della patria from
                                            "Andrea"
Massenet   Vision Fugitive from "Herodiade"
Rossini   Largo al factotum from "Barber
                                            of Seville"
Moussorgsky   To the Little Star
Gorin, Igor   Caucasian Melody
Verdi   Eri to from "Masked Ball"
Verdi   Credo from "Otello"
Kodaly   Dances from Galanta

January 22, 1959
Louis Kentner, *Pianist*

Bach-Cailliet   Toccata and Fugue in D Minor
Beethoven   Concerto No. 5
Brahms   Symphony No. 3

February 5, 1959
Alphonse Carlo, *Violinist;* Geraldine Gee, *Violist;* Manly Duckworth,

158

Pianist; Eugene Johnson, *Flutist*

Ibert	Suite Elizabethean
Mendelssohn	Concerto No. 1
Griffes	Poem for Flute
Mozart	Sinfonia Concertante for Violin *and* Viola, K. 364

February 19 and 21, 1959
Alphonse Carlo, *Violinist*

Read, Gardner	First Overture
Lalo	Symphonie Espagnole
Copland	Appalachian Spring
Gould	Spirituals

March 5, 1959
Victoria de los Angeles, *Soprano*

Mendelssohn	Symphony No. 4
Mozart	Motet for Soprano, K. 165, Exultate Jub'te
Boito	L'latra notte in fondo from "Mefistofele"
Rossini	Una voce poco fa from "Barber of Seville"
Gounod	Il etait un roi de Thule, and Je ris de me voir se belle from "Faust"
Ravel	Menuet Antique
Liszt	Les Preludes

March 12, 1959
Virginia Bradbury, *Soprano;* Jevne Kessel, *Mezzo-soprano;* Symphony Women's Chorus, Edna Johnston, Director

R. Strauss	Macbeth
Debussy	Three Nocturnes
Gustave Soderland	Festival
Debussy	La Damoiselle Elue
Balakirev	"Islamey's" Oriental Fantasy

March 19, 1959
Jorge Bolet, *Pianist*

Rossini	Italian in Algiers Overture
Rachmaninoff	Concerto No. 3
Liszt	Mephisto Waltz
Albeniz	Fete Dieu a Seville
R. Strauss	Death and Transfiguration

SEASON: 1959-60   CONDUCTOR: Henry Mazer

OFFICERS & MEMBERS OF EXECUTIVE COMMITTEE
GEORGE W. JOHNSON .... Chairman of the Board

MISS HELEN RYAN .... President
DR. A. H. SPIVACK .... First Vice President
MRS. LEONARD DYER .... Second Vice President

159

TENTH SEASON 1959-60

January 7, 1960

Handel -Harty	Water Music Suite
Wagner	Prelude and Libestod from Tristan *and* Isolde"
Tchaikovsky	Symphony No. 5

January 14, 1960
Arthur Gold and Robert Fizdale, *Pianists*

Bartok	Roumanian Folk Dances
Brahms	Symphony No. 4
Mozart	Concerto for Two Pianos, K. 365
Poulenc	Concerto for Two Pianos

January 28, 1960
Leonard Warren, *Baritone*

Schubert	Symphony No. 8
Ravel	Don Quichotte a dulcinee
Verdi	Credo from "Otello"
Prokofiev	Three Movements from Lt. Kije Suite
Gounod	Avant de quitter ces lieux from "Faust'
Verdi	E. Sogno? a realta? from "Falstaff"
Barber	Overture to School for Scandal

February 4, 1960
Katherine Carlo, *Pianist*

Handel	Concerto Grosso in D
d'Indy	Symphony on a French Mountain Air
Berlioz	Symphonie Fantastique

February 18 and 20, 1960
Alphonse Carlo, *Violinist*

Stravinsky	Pulcinella
Saint-Saens	Concerto in B Minor
Beethoven	Symphony No. 3

March 3, 1960
FSO Principals

Mozart	Sinfonia Concertante for Oboe, Clarinet, Horn, and Bassoon
Beethoven	Leonore Overture No. 3
Sibelius	Symphony No. 2

March 10, 1960
Leonard Pennario, *Pianist*

Rossini	Barber of Seville Overture
Schumann	Concerto in A Minor
Shostakovich	Symphony No. 5

March 24, 1960
Eileen Farrell, *Soprano*

Mozart	Symphony No. 38
Gluck	Divinites do Styx from "Alceste"
Debussy	Air de lia from L'Enfant prodique
Wagner	Ride of the Walkuries
Wagner	Siegfried's Funeral Music
Wagner	Brunhilde's Immolation Scene

SEASON: 1960-61   CONDUCTOR: Henry Mazer

OFFICERS & MEMBERS OF EXECUTIVE COMMITTEE

FRED G. TEGDER .... Chairman of the Board

GEORGE W. JOHNSON .... President
MISS HELEN E. RYAN .... Executive Vice-President
DR. A. H. SPIVACK .... First Vice-President
MRS. LEONARD DYER .... Second Vice-President
MRS. ELWYN EVANS .... Secretary
MRS. JOHN W. FREEMAN .... Assistant Secretary
GEORGE BAER .... Treasurer
FREDERICK W. SLEIGHT .... Assistant Treasurer

Judge John G. Baker	Mrs. R. D. Keene
Mrs. F. Page Bussells	Mrs. Loomis C. Leedy
Dr. Harold Gleason	John Masek
J. Edward Greaves	Miss Margaret Piper
Miss Joy Hawley	James A. Pittman
Harrison Hollander	F. Burton Smith
Mrs. Walter B. Johnston	John Tiedtke

BUDGET: $145,029 LENGTH OF SEASON 12 Weeks # MUSICIANS: 66

PRESIDENT OF WOMEN'S COMMITTEE: Mrs. Richard Chace
PRESIDENT OF ASSOCIATE BOARD: John A. Baker

ELEVENTH SEASON 1960-61

January 5, 1961

Berlioz	Roman Carnival Overture
Beethoven	Symphony No. 6
Delius	Walk to the Paradise Garden
R. Strauss	Suite from Der Rosenkavalier

January 12, 1961
Leonard Rose, *Cellist*

Bach	Sheep May Safely Graze
Brahms	Symphony No. 1
Kubik, Gail	Folk Song Suite
Bloch	Schelomo

January 26, 1961
John Browning, *Pianist*

Wagner	Prelude, Dance of Apprentices, *and* Act III Finale from "Die Meistersinger"
Shostakovich	Symphony No. 1
Mozart	Concerto No. 14 in Eb, K. 449
Ravel	Piano Concerto for Left Hand

February 2, 1961

Stravinsky	Divertimento, Fairy's Kiss
Ibert	Escales (Ports of Call)
Tchaikovsky	Symphony No. 4

February 16, 1961

Haydn	Symphony No. 100
De Falla	Three Dances from "Three-Cornered Hat"
Bach	Brandenburg Concerto No. 5
Respighi	Pines of Rome

March 9, 1961
Berl Senofsky, *Violinist*

Verdi	La Forza del Destino Overture
Hindemith	Mathis der Maler
Brahms	Violin Concerto

March 16, 1961
Eddy Manson, Guest Conductor

Milhaud	Le Boeuf sur le Toit
Barlow, Wayne	Rhapsody "The Winter's Part" for Oboe and Orchestra
Manson, Eddy	Symphony No. 1
Rimsky-Korsakov	Scheherazade

March 23, 1961
Alexander Bloch, *Guest Conductor*
Saramae Endich, *Soprano;* Jane Hobson, *Contralto;* David Lloyd, *Tenor;* Donald Gramm, *Bass;* Bach Festival Choir

Vitali-Charlier	Chaconne
Beethoven	Symphony No. 9

SEASON: 1961-62   CONDUCTOR: Henry Mazer

OFFICERS & MEMBERS OF EXECUTIVE COMMITTEE

FRED G. TEGDER .... Chairman of the Board

GEORGE W. JOHNSON. .... President

BUDGET $163,500 LENGTH OF SEASON: 14 Weeks # MUSICIANS: 66

PRESIDENT OF WOMEN'S COMMITTEE: Mrs. Arnold J. Wilson, Jr.
PRESIDENT OF ASSOCIATE BOARD: D. Arthur Yergey

TWELFTH SEASON 1961-62

January 4, 1962

Rossini	La Cenerentola Overture
Brahms	Symphony No. 3
Vaughn-Williams	Fantasia on a Theme of Tallis
Ravel	Daphnis et Chloe No. 2 Suite

January 11, 1962

Weber	Oberon Overture
Franck	Symphony in D Minor
Moussorgsky	Pictures At An Exhibition

January 18, 1962
Marguerite Haldeman and Alphonse Carlo, *Violinists*

Bernstein	Candide Overture
Prokofiev	Symphony No. 5
Bach	Concerto for Two Violins in D Minor
Smetana	Die Moldau

January 25, 1962
Van Cliburn, *Pianist*

Tchaikovsky	Capriccio Italien
Tchaikovsky	Romeo and Juliet
Tchaikovsky	Concerto No. 1

February 15, 1962
Aaron Rosand, *Violinist*

Lester Trimble	Five Episodes (Commissioned by FSO)
Stravinsky	Petrouchka Suite
Mendelssohn	Violin Concerto
Wagner	Tannhauser Overture

163

March 8, 1962
Maureen Forrester, *Contralto*

Mozart	Symphony No. 38
Mahler	Songs of a Wayfarer
De Falla	El Amor Brujo
Rimsky-Korsakov	Russian Easter Overture

March 22, 1962
David Everhart, *Cellist*

Brahms	Academic Festival Overture
Beethoven	Symphony No. 5
Saint-Saens	Concerto for Cello in A Minor
Debussy	La Mer

April 6, 1962
Bach Festival Choir; Marion Vincent, *Soprano;* Joy Davidson, *Contralto;* John McCollum,*Tenor;* Martin Gabel, Narrator

Haydn	Symphony No. 102
Honegger	King David

SEASON: 1962-63   CONDUCTOR: Henry Mazer
OFFICERS & MEMBERS OF EXECUTIVE COMMITTEE

JUDGE JOHN G. BAKER .... Chairman of the Board

GEORGE W. JOHNSON .... President
MISS HELEN E. RYAN .... Executive Vice-President
DR. A. H. SPIVACK .... First Vice-President
MRS. LEONARD DYER .... Second Vice-President
MRS. ELWYN EVANS .... Secretary
MRS. JOHN W. FREEMAN .... Assistant Secretary
GEORGE J. BAER .... Treasurer
FREDERICK W. SLEIGHT .... Assistant Treasurer

Robert T. Anderson	John Tiedtke	Eric Ravndal
John A. Baker	Mrs. Walter B. Johnston	F. D. Streep, Jr.
Henry Cragg	Mrs. Loomis C. Leedy	Mrs. Fred G. Tegder, Jr.
Dr. Harold Gleason	Mrs. McCullough Maguire	Mrs. Arnold W. Wilson, Jr.
Miss Joy Hawley	John Masek	
Harrison Hollander	Miss Margaret Piper	

BUDGET: $170,811   LENGTH OF SEASON: 14 Weeks   # MUSICANS: 66

PRESIDENT OF WOMEN'S COMMITTEE: Mrs. Arnold J. Wilson, Jr.
PRESIDENT OF ASSOCIATE BOARD: Nils Schweizer

THIRTEENTH SEASON 1962-63

January 3, 1963

Wagner	Prelude to Act III, Lohengrin
Beethoven	Symphony No. 7
Debussy	Prelude to Afternoon of a Faun
Stravinsky	Firebird Suite

January 17, 1963
John Frusciante, *Pianist*

Mendelssohn	Fingal's Cave Overture

| Grieg | Piano Concerto |
| Prokofiev | Ballet Suite, Romeo and Juliet |

January 24, 1963
Alfred Wallenstein, *Guest Conductor*

Brahms	Tragic Overture
Brahms	Symphony No. 2
Brahms	Variations on a Theme of Haydn
Brahms	Hungarian Dances

January 31, 1963
Sidney Harth, Violinist

Mozart	Marriage of Figaro Overture
Beethoven	Violin Concerto
Boda, John	Overture 1962 (Commissioned by FSO)
Debussy	Iberia, No. 2 of Images

February 14, 1963
Rudolf Firkusny, *Pianist*

Bartok	Concerto for Orchestra
Mozart	Serenade No. 6 for 2 small orchestras in D, K. 239
Beethoven	Concerto No. 3

March 7, 1963
Marguerite Haldeman, *Violinist*
Donald Morehead, *Percussionist*

Milhaud	Concerto for Percussion
Walton	Violin Concerto
Rossini	Overture to La Gazza Ladra
Respighi	Pines of Rome

March 28, 1963
Lorin Hollander, *Pianist*

| Tchaikovsky | Symphony No. 6 |
| Khachaturian | Piano Concerto |

April 5, 1963
Phyllis Curtin, *Soprano;* Florence Kopleff, *Mezzo-soprano;* John McCollum, *Tenor;* Kenneth Smith, *Bass;* Bach Festival Choir

| Haydn | Symphony No. 104 |
| Verdi | Requiem |

SEASON: 1963-64   CONDUCTOR: Henry Mazer

OFFICERS & MEMBERS OF EXECUTIVE COMMITTEE

ROBERT T. ANDERSON .... President
MISS HELEN E. RYAN .... Executive Vice-President
DR. A. H. SPIVACK .... Vice-President
MRS. LEONARD DYER .... Vice-President
MRS. A. J. WILSON, JR. .... Vice-President
JOHN A. BAKER .... Vice President
MRS. ELWYN EVANS .... Secretary

BUDGET: $196,409 LENGTH OF SEASON: 16 Weeks # MUSICIANS:66

PRESIDENT OF WOMEN'S COMMITTEE: Mrs. William Ellis
PRESIDENT OF ASSOCIATE BOARD: Tedford Eidson

FOURTEENTH SEASON 1963-64

December 19, 1963

Beethoven	Symphony No. 3
Barber	Adagio for Strings
Tchaikovsky	Francesca da Rimini

January 9, 1964
Alphonse Carlo, *Violinist*
Thomas Brockman, *Pianist*

Prokofiev	Classical Symphony
Khachaturian	Violin Concerto
Chopin	Piano Concerto No. 2
Berlioz	Three Excerpts from "Damnation of Faust"

January 23, 1964

Strauss, R.	Le Bourgeouis Gentilhomme Suite
Brahms	Symphony No. 4

January 30, 1964
Cesare Siepi, *Bass*

Barbirolli	Elizabethan Suite
Mozart	Non piu andrai, and Aprite un po' quege' Occhi madamina from "Don Giovanni"
Rossini	La Scala di Seta Overture
Poulenc	Suite from ballet Les Biches
Ravel	Don Quichotte e dulcinee
Gounod	Mefistofele's Serenade from "Faust"

March 5, 1964
Van Cliburn, *Pianist*

Rossini	Italian in Algiers Overture
Mendelssohn	Symphony No. 4
Brahms	Concerto No. 2

March 12, 1964
Joe Kreines, Guest Conductor

Rachmaninoff	Symphony No. 2
Ives	Three Places in New England (Conducted by Kreines)

166

Strauss, R.	Don Juan

March 19, 1964
Isaac Stern, *Violinist*

Hindemith	Symphonic Metamorphosis on Weber Themes
Bruch	Violin Concerto No. 1
Mozart	Concerto in G, K. 216
Wagner	Prelude to Die Meistersinger

April 3, 1964
Irene Jordan, *Soprano;* Florence Kopleff, *Contralto,* Jon Crain, *Tenor;* Donald Gramm, *Bass;* Bach Festival Choir

Beethoven	Leonore Overture No. 3
Beethoven	Abscheulicher, wo irlst du hin? from "Fidelio" (sung by Jordan)
Beethoven	Symphony No. 9

SEASON: 1964-65   CONDUCTOR: Henry Mazer

OFFICERS & MEMBERS OF EXECUTIVE COMMITTEE

ROBERT T. ANDERSON .... President
MISS HELEN E. RYAN .... Executive Vice-President
MRS. LEONARD DYER .... Vice President
MRS. A. J. WILSON, JR. .... Vice-President
JOHN A. BAKER .... Vice President
GEORGE J. BAER .... Treasurer

William J. Bowen	Craig Linton	Mrs. Fred G. Tegder
George S. Bradshaw	Mrs. McCullough Maguire	John Tiedtke
Thomas Fuller	Benjamin H. Oehlert, Jr.	J. Walter Tucker
George W. Johnson	Miss Margaret Piper	Clyde A. West
Mrs. Loomis C. Leedy	F. Burton Smith	Mrs. G. T. Willey

BUDGET: $220,510 LENGTH OF SEASON: 17 Weeks # MUSICIANS: 66

PRESIDENT OF WOMENS COMMITTEE: Mrs. William N. Ellis
PRESIDENT OF ASSOCIATE BOARD: Joseph Culp

FIFTEENTH SEASON 1964-65

December 10, 1964

Mendelssohn	Excerpts from Midsummer Night's Dream
Debussy	Two Nocturnes
Shostakovich	Symphony No. 5

December 17, 1965
George London, *Baritone;* Martinaires (Martin Company Chorus)

Mozart	Divertimento No. 17, K. 334 in D
Strauss	Dance of Seven Veils from "Salome"
Moussorgsky	Excerpts from Boris Godounov

January 7, 1965
Eileen Farrell, *Soprano*

Wagner	Rienzi Overture

Wagner	Five Songs
Harris, Roy	Symphony No. 3
Mascagni	Voi lo sapete from "Cavalleria Rusticana"
Verdi	Ernani involami from "Ernani"

January 21, 1965
Leon Fleisher, *Pianist*

Vaughan-Williams	Symphony No. 5
Mozart	Concerto No. 25
Rachmininoff	Rhapsody on a Theme of Paganini

February 4, 1965
Ruggiero Ricci, *Violinist*

Tchaikovsky	Waltz from Eugene Onegin
Tchaikovsky	Violin Concerto
Tchaikovsky	Symphony No. 5

March 13, 1965
E. Power Biggs, *Organist*

Handel	Concerto for Organ No. 13 in F
Poulenc	Concerto for Organ, Strings, and Tympani
Saint-Saens	Symphony No. 3

March 25, 1965
Richard Burgin, *Guest Conductor*

Sibelius	Symphony No. 1
Copland	Music for the Theatre
Rimsky-Korsakov	Suite for "Tsar Saltan"

April 2, 1965
Felicia Montealegre and Michael Wager, *Narrators;* Lois Marshall, *Soprano;* Jane Hobson, *Contralto;* David Lloyd, *Tenor;* Ken Smith, *Bass;* Alice Hufstader, *incidental solo* and *speaking part;* Robert Arel, William Hardy and H. E. McFarland, *incidental speaking part;* 'Bach Festival Choir; Rock Lake Elementary Chorus

Bach	Suite No. 2 in B Minor
Honegger	Jeanne d'Arc au Bucher

SEASON: 1965-66   CONDUCTOR: Henry Mazer

OFFICERS & MEMBERS OF EXECUTIVE COMMITTEE

ROBERT T. ANDERSON .... President
MISS HELEN E. RYAN .... Executive Vice President
MRS. LEONARD DYER .... Vice President
MRS. A. J. WILSON, JR. .... Vice President
JOHN A. BAKER .... Vice President
GEORGE J. BAER .... Treasurer

Mrs. B. L. Abberger, Jr.	Mrs. Luther K. Jennings	George W. Johnson
William J. Bowen	Mrs. Loomis C. Leedy	F. Burton Smith
George S. Bradshaw	Craig Linton	Mrs. Grant Staton
Mrs. Robert Doenges	Mrs. McCullough Maguire	Mrs. Fred G. Tegder
Mrs. William N. Ellis	Mrs. Robert Neel	John Tiedtke
Thomas H. Fuller	Miss Margaret Piper	J. Walter Tucker

Harry Phipps   Clyde A. West
Fred Peirsol   Mrs. G. T. Willey

BUDGET: $243,475 LENGTH OF SEASON:17 Weeks # MUSICIANS: 66

PRESIDENT OF WOMEN'S COMMITTEE: Mrs. Luther Jennings
PRESIDENT OF ASSOCIATE BOARD: Harry Phipps

SIXTEENTH SEASON 1965-66

December 16, 1965
Doris Yarick, *Soprano;* Dorothy Hepburn, *Mezzo-soprano;* John Mc
Collum, *Tenor;* William Warfield, Baritone; combined Orlando area
church choirs; Phyllis Bleck and David Justis, *Trumpeters [FSO]*

Vivaldi	Concerto for Two Trumpets
Handel	Excerpts from "Messiah"

January 6, 1966

Berlioz	Roman Carnival Overture
Beethoven	Symphony No. 5
Respighi	The Birds
Stravinsky	Suite from Fire Bird

January 20, 1966
Leonard Rose, *Cellist*

Morawetz, Oscar	Passacaglia on Bach Chorale
Dvorak	Cello Concerto
Kodaly	Hary Janos Suite

January 27, 1966
Nicanor Zabaleta, *Harpist*

Schubert	Symphony No. 2
Boieldieu	Concerto for Harp
Ravel	Death and Transfiguration

February 3, 1966
Yuri Krasnopolsky, *Guest Conductor*
Phillippe Entremont, *Pianist*

Dvorak	Carnival Overture
Beethoven	Concerto No. 4
Brahms	Symphony No. 1

March 17, 1966
Gina Bachauer, *Pianist*

Gabrieli	Sonata pian e forte from Sacrae Symphoniae
Prokofiev	Concerto No. 3
Moussorgsky	Pictures At An Exhibition

March 24, 1966
Natasha Kimmel, *Mezzo-soprano*
Fritz Siegel, *Violinist*

Mozart	Symphony No. 36
Sibelius	Violin Concerto
Bernstein	Symphony Jeremiah
Kabalevsky	Colas Breugnon Overture

169

April 11, 1966
Birgit Nilsson, *Soprano*

Stravinsky	Divertimento, The Fairy's Kiss
Wagner	Elsa's Dream from "Lohengrin"
Wagner	Love Death from "Tristan und Isolde"
Verdi	Nile Scene from "Aida"
Verdi	Pace, pace, mio dio from "La Forza del Destino"
Rimsky-Korsakov	Capriccio Espagnole

SEASON: 1966-67   GUEST CONDUCTORS

OFFICERS & MEMBERS OF EXECUTIVE COMMITTEE

CRAIG LINTON .... President
MISS HELEN E. RYAN .... Executive V. President
GEORGE B. GIBSON .... Vice President
JOHN A. BAKER .... Vice President
MRS. S. G. LATTY .... Secretary
JOHN TIEDTKE .... Treasurer

Mrs. B. L. Abberger	Frederick W. Peirsol
Mrs. Nelson Boice	Anthony Ponticelli
Mrs. William Daniel	J. Walter Tucker
Mrs. Luther Jennings	Mrs. Thomas Vickers
George W. Johnson	Henry A. White

BUDGET: $243,069 LENGTH OF SEASON: 17 Weeks # MUSICIANS: 66

PRESIDENT OF WOMEN'S COMMITTEE: Mrs. Thomas Vickers
PRESIDENT OF ASSOCIATE BOARD: Frederick W. Peirsol
PRESIDENT OF OPERA GALA GUILD: Mrs. William R. Daniel

SEVENTEENTH SEASON 1966-67

December 29, 1966
Yuri Krasnopolsky, *Conductor*

Wagner	Prelude to Die Meistersinger
Haydn	Symphony No. 88
De Falla	Three Dances from "Three-Cornered Hat"
Sibelius	Symphony No. 2

January 5, 1967
Yuri Krasnopolsky, *Conductor*

Beethoven	Egmont Overture
Bartok	Hungarian Peasant Songs
Ravel	Rapsodie Espagnole
Tchaikovsky	Symphony No. 4

January 19, 1967
Minas Christian, *Conductor*
Phyllis Curtin, *Soprano*

Handel-Kindler	Prelude and Fugue in D Minor

Mozart	Symphony No. 29
Ravel	Sheherazade
Barber	Music for a Scene from Shelley
Charpentier	Depuis le jour from "Louise"
Massenet	Adieu, notre petite table from "Manon"
Massenet	Recitative and Gavotte from "Manon"
Enesco	Roumanian Rhapsody No. 1

January 26, 1967
George Trautwein, *Conductor*
Edith Peinemann, Violinist

Beethoven	Leonore Overture No. 2
Bartok	Concerto for Violin
Dvorak	Symphony No. 9, New World

March 16, 1967
Joseph Levine, Conductor
Julius Katchen, *Pianist*

Haydn	Symphony No. 31, Horn Signal
Menotti	Sebastian Ballet Suite
Brahms	Concerto for Piano No. 1

March 30, 1967
Hermann Herz, Conductor

Weber	Der Freischutz Overture
Schumann	Symphony No. 1
Prokofiev	Symphony No. 5

April 7, 1967
Hermann Herz, *Conductor*

Handel	Suite from Faithful Shepherd
Mozart	Symphony No. 40
Milhaud	Suite Provencale
Griffes	White Peacock
Walton	Johannesburg Festival Overture

April 14, 1967
Yuri Krasnopolsky, *Conductor*
William Steck, *Violinist;* Yuan Tung, *Cellist;* Yuri Krasnopolksy,
Pianist; Bach Festival Choir; Diane Bentley, *Soprano;* Eleanor
Gronlund, *Alto;* Arthur Hammond, *Tenor;* Miles Williams, *Bass*

Mozart	Marriage of Figaro Overture
Beethoven	Triple Concerto
Kodaly	Te Deum
Britten	Variations and Fugue on Theme of Purcell

SEASON: 1967-68   CONDUCTOR: Hermann Herz

OFFICERS & MEMBERS OF EXECUTIVE COMMITTEE

CRAIG LINTON .... President

EIGHTEENTH SEASON 1967-68

December 14, 1967

Mozart	Magic Flute Overture
Brahms	Symphony No. 2
Respighi	Fountains of Rome
Weinberger	Polka and Fugue from "Schwanda the Bagpiper"

December 28, 1967
David Bar-Illan, *Pianist*

Hovaness	Mysterious Mountain
Mozart	Concertino in D
Mendelssohn	Concerto No. 1 for Piano
Franck	Symphony in D Minor

January 18, 1968
James Gilbertsen, *Trombonist*

Giannini	Frescobaldiana
Debussy	Prelude to Afternoon of a Faun
Creston	Fantasy for Trombone
Schubert	Symphony No. 9

February 15, 1968
Leslie Parnas, *Cellist*

Gutche	Hsiang Fei
Bloch	Schelomo
Tchaikovsky	Symphony No. 6

March 14, 1968

Barber	School for Scandal Overture
Nielsen	Symphony No. 5
Tchaikovsky	Serenade for Strings
Dvorak	Slavonic Dances No. 2 and 3

April 4, 1968
Esther Glazer, Violinist

Beethoven	Coriolanus Overture

172

Beethoven	Symphony No. 6
Paganini	Concerto No. 1
Ravel	La Valse

April 18, 1968
Abbey Simon, *Pianist*

Strauss	Don Juan
Shostakovich	Symphony No. 9
Brahms	Concerto No. 2 for Piano

April 26, 1968
Diane Bentley, *Soprano;* John Fiorito, *Baritone;* Camerata Chorus
and Bach Festival Chorus

Poulenc	Gloria (Camerata and Bentley)
Orff	Carmina Burana (Bach, Bentley, and Fiorito)

SEASON: 1968-69   CONDUCTOR: Hermann Herz

OFFICERS & MEMBERS OF EXECUTIVE COMMITTEE

GEORGE B. GIBSON .... President
MISS HELEN E. RYAN .... Executive Vice President
W. R. WINN, JR. .... Vice President
DR. JAMES B. DINNEEN................... Second Vice President
NILS SCHWEIZER, ... Third Vice President
MRS. WILLIAM DANIEL .... Secretary
JOHN TIEDTKE .... Treasurer

Stephen Dean	Craig Linton
George Eidson, Jr.	Mrs. Gene Rich
Mrs. Cloyde Fausnaugh	F. D. Streep, Jr.
Charles Fratt	MacDonnell Tyre
Mrs. Charles Fratt	William Webster
Mrs. Jack Hudson	Clyde A. West
Mrs. Walter B. Johnston	Mrs. A. J. Wilson, Jr.

BUDGET: $331,467 LENGTH OF SEASON: 20 Weeks # MUSICIANS: 73

PRESIDENT OF WOMEN'S COMMITTEE: Mrs. Jack Hudson
PRESIDENT OF ASSOCIATE BOARD: Rodney Kincaid
PRESIDENT OF OPERA GALA GUILD: Mrs. Gene Rich

NINETEENTH SEASON 1968-69

December 19, 1968
Gwendolyn Killebrew, *Soprano;* John Stewart, *Tenor;* Kenneth
Smith, *Bass;* and *Camerata Chorus*

Wagner	Rienzi Overture
Wagner	Prelude and Dance of Apprentices
Wagner	Finale to Act III from "Die Meistersinger"
Vaughan-Williams	Hodie, A Christmas Cantata

December 26, 1968
Janet Mascaro, *Oboeist*

Verdi	Vespri Siciliani Overture

Dvorak	Symphony No. 8
Handel	Oboe Concerto No. 1
Delius	Walk to Paradise Garden
Strauss, R.	Der Rosenkavalier Waltzes

January 9, 1969
Teresa Stratas, *Soprano*

Mendelssohn	Fingal's Cave Overture
Barber	Symphony No. 8
Tchaikovsky	Letter Scene from "Eugene Onegin"
Mozart	Voi che sapete and Non so piu from "Marriage of Figaro"
Verdi	Pace, pace mio dio from "La Forza del Destino"
Albeniz-Arbos	Triana and Fete dieu a Seville from "Iberia"

January 23, 1969
Pavle Despalj, *Conductor*
Bernard Parronchi, *Cellist*

Nielsen	Helios Overture
Boccherini	Cello Concerto in Bb
Brahms	Symphony No. 4

February 18, 1969
Pavle Despalj, *Conductor*
Uto Ughi, *Violinist*

Tchaikovsky	Romeo and Juliet Overture
Bruch	Violin Concerto No. 1
Saint-Saens	Introduction and Rondo Capriccioso
Ravel	Daphnis and Chloe Suite No. 2

March 20, 1969
Byron Janis, *Pianist*

Rimsky-Korsakov	Russian Easter Overture
Prokofiev	Symphony No. 7
Tchaikovsky	Piano Concerto No. 1

April 17, 1969
Gary Graffman, *Pianist*

Mozart	Serenade No. 6
Schumann	Piano Concerto in A Minor
Mahler	Symphony No. 1

April 24, 1969
Florida Youth Symphony, *guest artists*

Milhaud	Suite Francaise
Bizet	Symphony No. 1

Florida Youth Symphony

Frescobaldi-Kindler	Toccata
Delibes	March and Procession of Bacchus from "Sylvia"
Respighi	Pines of Rome

174

SEASON: 1969-70   CONDUCTOR: Hermann Herz

OFFICERS & MEMBERS OF EXECUTIVE COMMITTEE

GEORGE B. GIBSON	President
MISS HELEN E. RYAN	Executive Vice President
W. R. WINN, JR.	Vice President
NILS SCHWEIZER	Vice President
MRS. WILLIAM DANIEL, ...	Secretary
CHARLES FRATT	Treasurer

Robert T. Anderson   Hugh Jones, Jr.
Stephen Dean   Craig Linton
Mrs. Cloyde Fausnaugh   Frederick W. Peirsol
Ronald A. Harbert   Mrs. Glen Pierson, Jr.
Mrs. Robert Hughes   Alfred Shepard
Mrs. Luther Jennings   F. D. Streep, Jr.
                            Clyde A. West

BUDGET: $367,142 LENGTH OF SEASON: 20 Weeks # MUSICIANS: 73

PRESIDENT OF WOMEN'S COMMITTEE: Mrs. Rita B. Pierson
PRESIDENT OF ASSOCIATE BOARD: Hugh J. Jones, Jr.
PRESIDENT OF OPERA GALA GUILD: Mrs. Robert Hughes

TWENTIETH SEASON 1969-70

December 18, 1969

Weber	Euryanthe Overture
Wagner	Forest Murmurs from "Siegfried"
Dvorak	Scherzo Capriccioso
Tchaikovsky	Symphony No. 5 in E, Op. 64

January 8, 1970
Pavle Despalj, *Conductor*
Sidney Harth, *Violinist*

Brahms	Academic Festival Overture
Brahms	Concerto in D for Violin, Op. 77
Brahms	Symphony No. 1 in C, Op. 68

January 22, 1970

Beethoven	Fidelio Overture
Schumann-Mahler	Symphony No. 3 in Eb, Op. 97
Ravel	Introduction and Allegro for Harp
Sibelius	Swan of Tuonela
Grieg	Norwegian Dances

February 12, 1970
Van Cliburn, *Pianist*

Rimsky-Korsakov	Capriccio Espagnol, Op. 34
MacDowell	Concerto No. 2 in D for Piano, Op. 23
Rachmaninoff	Concerto No. 2 in C for Piano, Op. 38

March 12, 1970
Pavle Despalj, *Conductor*
Majda Despalj, *Mezzo-soprano*

Handel	Overture to Jephtha
Gluck	Orpheus:
	No. 28 Furientanz
	No. 6 Ritornell
	No. 7, 8, 9 Aria, Recitative, Aria
	No. 30 Ballett
	No. 42, 43 Recitative and Aria
	Barbiere de Sevilla:
	Uvertira
	Recitativo and Cavantina do
	Rosina
Strauss	Death and Transfiguration, Op. 24
Wagner	Prelude and Liebestod from
	"Tristan und Isolde"

March 30, 1970
Susan Harris, *Piccolo*

Walton	Partita
Liadov	Enchanted Lake
Vivaldi	Concerto for Piccolo
Saint-Saens	Symphony No. 3 in C, Op. 78

April 9, 1970
Janet Mascaro, *Oboe*
Peter Harris, *Clarinet*
Arnold Mascaro, *Horn*
John Beck, *Bassoon*

Wagner	Overture to "The Flying
	Dutchman"
Mozart	Sinfonia Concertante in Eb for
	Oboe, Clarinet, Horn, and Bassoon
Shostakovich	Symphony No. 5, Op. 47

April 23, 1970
David Bar-Illan, *Pianist*

Mendelssohn	Symphony No. 4 in A, Op. 90
Chopin	Concerto No. 2 for Piano in F
Borodin	Polovetzian Dances
Liszt	Concerto No. 1 for Piano in Eb

SEASON: 1970-71   CONDUCTOR: Pavle Despalj

OFFICERS & MEMBERS OF EXECUTIVE COMMITTEE

F. D. STREEP JR. . . . . President
MISS HELEN E. RYAN . . . . Executive Vice-President
STEPHEN T. DEAN . . . . Vice-President
MRS. LUTHER JENNINGS . . . . Secretary
HUGH J. JONES, JR. . . . . Treasurer

Howard L. H. Gordon	Nils Schweizer
Robert L. Landers	MacDonnell Tyre
Mrs. Julian Pace	Floyd Winfree
Frederick W. Peirsol	Mrs. Ward Woodbury

BUDGET: $367,036 LENGTH OF SEASON: 20 Weeks # MUSICIANS: 73

PRESIDENT OF WOMEN'S COMMITTEE: Mrs. Ward Woodbury
PRESIDENT OF ASSOCIATE BOARD: Hugh J. Jones, Jr.
PRESIDENT OF OPERA GALA GUILD: Mrs. Julian Pace

TWENTY-FIRST SEASON 1970-71

December 17, 1970
Alphonse Carlo, *Violinist*

Beethoven	Egmont Overture
Beethoven	Concerto for Violin in D, Op. 61
Beethoven	Symphony No. 7 in A, Op. 92

January 7, 1971
Lorin Hollander, *Pianist*

Brahms	Symphony No. 3 in F, Op. 90
Strauss	Burleske for Piano and Orchestra
Rachmaninoff	Rhapsody on a Theme of Paganini

January 14, 1971
Majda Despalj, *Mezzo-soprano*

Barber	Second Essay
De Falla	El Amor Brujo
Tchaikovsky	Symphony No. 4 in F, Op.36

January 28, 1971
Itzhak Perlman, *Violinist*

Bach	Brandenburg Concerto No. 1
Ives	Three Places in New England
Tchaikovsky	Concerto for Violin in D, Op. 35

March 11, 1971
Cecil Leeson, *Saxophonist*

Britten	Sinfonette
Despalj	Concerto for Saxophone
Berlioz	Symphonie Fantastique, Op. 14

March 18, 1971
Lili Kraus, *Pianist*

Hindemith	Symphonie Metamorphosis
Mozart	Concerto No. 23 in A for Piano, K-488
Beethoven	Concerto No. 3 in C for Piano, Op. 37

April 1, 1971
Arpad Szomoru, Cellist

Wagner	Tannhauser Overture
Saint-Saens	Concerto for Cello in A, Op.33
Strauss	Serenade for Winds
Sulek	Symphony No. 3

April 15, 1971

Stravinsky	Petrouchka
Ravel	Rapsodie Espagnole
Strauss	Till Eulenspiegel

177

SEASON: 1971-72   CONDUCTOR: Pavle Despalj

OFFICERS & MEMBERS OF EXECUTIVE COMMITTEE

STEPHEN T. DEAN .... President
MISS HELEN E. RYAN .... Executive Vice President
FREDERICK W. PEIRSOL .... Vice President
F. D. STREEP, JR. .... Vice President
BRUCE H. WELSH .... Vice President
MRS. LUTHER JENNINGS .... Vice President
MRS. NELSON BOICE, JR. .... Secretary
HUGH J. JONES, JR. .... Treasurer
F. D. STREEP, JR. .... Chairman of the Board

Bruce G. Blackman   Dr. Charles Micarelli
Mrs. Walter B. Johnston   Mrs. William G. Newsom, Jr.
Robert L. Landers   Mrs. Frederick W. Peirsol

BUDGET: $399,108 LENGTH OF SEASON: 22 Weeks ∦ MUSICIANS: 73

PRESIDENT OF WOMEN'S COMMITTEE: Mrs. Frederick W. Peirsol
PRESIDENT OF ASSOCIATE BOARD: Bruce Blackman
PRESIDENT OF OPERA GALA GUILD: Mrs. William Newsom

TWENTY-SECOND SEASON 1971-72

December 16, 1971
Linda Threatte, *Flutist*

Schumann	Manfred Overture
Ibert	Concerto for Flute
Beethoven	Symphony No. 3

January 6, 1972
Beverly Wolff, *Mezzo-soprano*

Brahms	Tragic Overture
Mahler	Kindertotenlieder
Despalj	Variations
Mozart	"Parto, parto, ma to ben mio"
Massenet	"Letter Aria"

January 20, 1972
Ivan Davis, *Pianist*

Bach	Brandenburg Concerto No. 3
Saint-Saens	Piano Concerto No. 4
Travis	Collage for Orchestra
Grieg	Piano Concerto

February 10, 1972
Yong Uck Kim, *Violinist*

Prokofiev	Suite No. 2 from the Ballet "Romeo and Juliet, Op. 64
Mozart	Concerto in A Major, No. 5, K. 219
Lalo	Symphoney Espagnole for Violin *and* Orchestra, Op. 21

March 9, 1972
Arnold Mascaro, *Hornist*

178

Haydn	Symphony No. 103
Strauss	Concerto No. 1 for Horn
Shostakovich	Symphony No. 1

March 16, 1972
Pierre Fournier, *Cellist*

| Bartok | Concerto for Orchestra |
| Dvorak | Concerto for Cello |

April 6, 1972
Garrick Ohlsson, *Pianist*

Floyd	Introduction, Aria and Dance
Ravel	Concerto for the Left Hand
Rachmaninoff	Concerto No. 3

April 27, 1972
Majda Despalj, *Mezzo-Soprano*

| Mahler | Symphony No. 4 |
| Debussey | La Mer |

SEASON: 1972-73   CONDUCTOR: Pavle Despalj

OFFICERS & MEMBERS OF EXECUTIVE COMMITTEE

STEPHEN T. DEAN .... President
WARREN R. WINN, JR. .... Vice President
JOSEPH WITTENSTEIN .... Vice President
MRS. EVE PROCTOR .... Vice President
MRS. LUTHER JENNINGS .... Vice President
MRS. NELSON R. BOICE, JR. .... Secretary
HUGH J. JONES, JR. .... Vice President and Treasurer
MISS HELEN E. RYAN .... Executive Vice President
ROBERT L. LANDERS .... Administrative Director
GEORGE B. GIBSON .... Chairman of the Board

Dr. David L. Evans	Mrs. Harry Phipps
Mrs. Walter B. Johnston	Mrs. Thomas Lineham
Dr. Charles Micarelli	Jack Glick
	MacDonnell Tyre

BUDGET: $462,438 LENGTH OF SEASON: 22 Weeks # MUSICIANS: 73

PRESIDENT OF WOMEN'S COMMITTEE: Mrs. Frederick W. Peirsol
PRESIDENT OF ASSOCIATE BOARD: Bruce G. Blackman
PRESIDENT OF OPERA GALA GUILD: Mrs. Harry W. Phipps

TWENTY-THIRD SEASON 1972-73

December 14, 1972
Peter Harris, *Clarinetist*

Weber	Overture to "Preciosa"
Brahms	Variations on a Theme by Joseph Haydn, Op. 56
Mozart	Concerto for Clarinet in A Major, K. 622

179

Beethoven	Symphony No. 5 in C Minor, Op. 67

January 11, 1973
LEONTYNE PRICE, *Soprano*

Mussorgsky-Ravel	Pictures at an Exhibition
Mozart	"Come Scoglio" (from Cosi Fan Tutti)
Verdi	"Ritorna vincitor" (from Aida)
Milhaud	The Creation of the World
Puccini	"Un bel di vedremo" (from Madama Butterfly)
Verdi	"Pace, pace mio Dio" (from La Forza del Destino)

February 8, 1973
Teiko Maehashi, *Violinist*

Wagner	Prelude to 'Die Meistersinger von Nurnberg'
Prokofiev	Concerto for Violin and Orchestra No. 1 in D Major, Op. 19
J. S. Bach	Concerto No. 2 in E Major for Violin & Orchestra
Stravinsky	The Firebird Suite

February 15, 1973
Lili Kraus, *Pianist*

Hindemith	Symphony 'Mathis Der Maler'
Weber	"Konzertstuck' for Piano and Orchestra, Op. 79
Beethoven	Concerto for Piano No. 4 in G Major, Op. 58

March 15, 1973
Erick Friedman, *Violinist*

Ives-Schuman	Variations on 'America'
DeFalla	Three Dances from the Ballet "The Three Cornered Hat"
Paganini	Concerto for Violin and Orchestra in D Major
Vieuxtemps	Concerto No. 5 in A Minor, Op. 37
Richard Strauss	"Don Juan"

March 29, 1973
The Philadelphia Orchestra
  Eugene Ormandy, *Conducting*

April 5, 1973
Alphonse Carlo, *Violinist*
Maja Vukovic, *Violinist*

Schuman	"New England Triptych"
K. Stamitz	Symphony Concertante for Two Violins and Orchestra

180

| *Tchaikovsky* | Symphony No. 6 in B Minor. |
| | Opus 74 (PATHETIQUE) |

April 19, 1973
Gary Graffman, *Pianist*

Prokofiev	Classical Symphony, Opus 25
Tchaikovsky	Concerto No. 3 in E Flat Major
	For Piano and Orchestra,
Brahms	Concerto for Piano & Orchestra
	No. 1 in D Minor, Opus 15

April 26, 1973
Katherine Carlo, *Pianist*

d'Indy	Symphony on a French Mountain
	Air, Opus 25
Bruckner	Symphony No. 7 in E Major

SEASON: 1973-74   CONDUCTOR: Pavle Despalj
OFFICERS & MEMBERS OF EXECUTIVE COMMITTEE

WARREN R. WINN, JR. .... President
HUGH J. JONES, JR. .... Vice President and Treasurer
MRS. EVE PROCTOR .... Vice President
DR. CHARLES MICARELLI .... Vice President
BRUCE G. BLACKMAN .... Vice President
MRS. W. G. NEWSOM JR. .... Secretary
STEPHEN T. DEAN .... Chairman of the Board

Robert L. Landers   Dr. David L. Evans
Claude Shivers   Miss Helen E. Ryan
Mrs. Robert Kolodney   Mrs. Meredith Gurney

BUDGET: $530,802 LENGTH OF SEASON: 23 Weeks # MUSICIANS: 75

PRESIDENT OF WOMEN'S COMMITTEE: Mrs. Robert Kolodney
PRESIDENT OF ASSOCIATE BOARD: Claude Shivers
PRESIDENT OF OPERA GALA GUILD: Mrs. Meredith Gurney

TWENTY-FOURTH SEASON 1973-74

December 13, 1973
Leonard Rose, *Cellist*

Strauss	Don Quixote
Schumann	Cello Concerto
Ravel	La Valse

January 3, 1974
Alphonse Carlo, *Violinist*

Bartok	Miraculous Mandarin Suite
Chausson	Poeme
Tschaikovsky	Symphony #5

January 10, 1974
Christian Zacharias, *Pianist*
   [Van Cliburn contest winner)

Wagner	Overture to Rienzi
Beethoven	Concerto for Piano & Orchestra in C Minor, No. 3, Opus 37
Barber	First Essay
Respighi	Pines of Rome

January 26, 1974
New York Philharmonic
  Morton Gould, *Conducting*

February 7, 1974
James Tocco, *Pianist*

Weber	Oberon Overture
Chopin	Piano Concerto No. 1
Stravinsky	Le Sacre Du Printemps

February 14, 1974
Dylana Jenson, *Violinist*

Mendelssohn	Midsummer Night's Dream Overture
Mendelssohn	Violin Concerto
Ives	Symphony No. 2

March 14, 1974
Richard Tucker, *Tenor*
Robert Merrill, *Baritone*

Britten	Four Sea Interludes from Peter Grimes
Mozart	Deh vieni alla finestra from Don Giovanni
Mozart	Non piu andrai from Le Nozze di Figaro
Puccini	Recondita Armonia from Tosca
Puccini	Nessun dorma from Turandot
Wagner	Prelude to Lohengrin
Ponchielli	Enzo Grimaldo from La Dioconda
Puccini	Intermezzo from Manon Lescaut
Puccini	No! Pazzo son, guardate! from Lescaut
Verdi	Credo from Otello
deFalla	Interlude and Dance from La Vida Breve
Verdi	Invano Alvaro from La Forza del Destino

March 28, 1974
Philippe Entremont, *Pianist*

Bloch	Trois Poemes Juifs
Prokofiev	Piano Concerto #3
Beethoven	Symphony No. 8

April 18, 1974
John Beck, *Bassoonist*

Kodaly	Dances of Galanta
Mozart	Bassoon Concerto
Brahms	Symphony No. 2

SEASON: 1974-75   CONDUCTOR: Pavle Despalj

OFFICERS & MEMBERS OF EXECUTIVE COMMITTEE

HUGH J. JONES, JR. .... President
BRUCE G. BLACKMAN .... Vice President
DR. DAVID L. EVANS .... Vice President
REID EWING .... Vice President
DR. CHARLES MICARELLI .... Vice President
HAROLD WARD, III .... Vice President
MRS. W. G. NEWSOM, JR. .... Secretary
HARRY A. SPEER .... Treasurer
WARREN R. WINN, JR. .... Chairman of the Board
MR. ROBERT L. LANDERS   Executive Vice President and General
                                                        Manager
MISS HELEN E. RYAN .... Manager of the Orchestra
MRS. B. L. ABBERGER, JR. .... President, Opera Gala Guild
MRS. PAUL HAYNE, JR. .... President, Women's Committee
MR. FRANK KANEY .... President, Associate Board

BUDGET: $623,866 LENGTH OF SEASON: 25 Weeks **#** MUSICIANS 75

PRESIDENT OF WOMEN'S COMMITTEE: Mrs. Paul Hayne, Jr.
PRESIDENT OF ASSOCIATE BOARD: Frank Kaney
PRESIDENT OF OPERA GALA GUILD: Mrs. Ben Abberger, Jr.

TWENTY-FIFTH SEASON 1974-75

December 5, 1974
Leontyne Price, *Soprano*

Tchaikovsky	1812 Overture (The Bach Festival Choir Ward Woodbury, Conductor)
Barber	Adagio for Strings, Opus 11
Mozart	D'Oreste, d'Ajace from Idomeneo
Verdi	Sorta e la notte . . . Ernani, Involami from Ernani
Handel	Royal Fireworks Music
Puccini	Tu, che di gel sei cinta from Turandot
Strauss	Zweite Brautnacht! from Die Aegyptische Helena

December 19, 1974
Janos Starker, *Cellist*

Blacher	Paganini Variations
Haydn	Cello Concerto in D Major
Franck	Symphony in D Minor

January 16, 1975
Maja Despalj, *Violinist*

Rossini	Semiramide Overture
Despalj:	*Violin Concerto
Dvorak:	Symphony No. 8

*American Premiere

183

January 30, 1975
The Florida Symphony

Bach	Suite #3 in D Major
Wagner	Prelude to Parsifal
Shostakovich	Symphony No. 5

January 30, 1975
Lorin Hollander, *Pianist*

Honegger	Pacific 231
Brahms	Piano Concerto No. 2
Elgar	Enigma Variations

March 13, 1975
Leon Bates, *Pianist*

Bernstein	Candide Overture
MacDowell	Piano Concerto No. 2
Gottschalk	Grand Tarantelle
Menotti	Triplo Concerto a Tre
Gershwin	American in Paris

March 27, 1975
Charles Gottschalk, *Trumpet Soloist*

Mozart	Haffner Symphony
Arutunian	Trumpet Concerto
Sibelius	Symphony No. 2

April 17, 1975
Itzhak Perlman, *Violinist*

Glinka	Russlan and Ludmilla Overture
Dvorak	Violin Concerto
Sulek	*Symphony No. 5

*American Premiere

May 4, 1975
The Cleveland Orchestra*
Lorin Maazel, *Conducting*

Barber	Overture to the School for Scandal
Debussy	Iberia
Tchaikovsky	Symphony No. 5

May 8, 1975
The Bach Festival Choir and Soloists

Beethoven	Leonora Overture #3
Beethoven	Symphony No. 9

Roberta Palmer, *Soprano*   Jack Trussel, *Tenor*
Pamela Gore, *Contralto*   Ronald Hedlund, *Baritone*

Though all officers and members of the executive committee of the Florida Symphony Society have been listed previously, the following also served as members (or honorary members) of the board of directors for varying periods during the past twenty-five years. To each of them — our gratitude.

A. N. Abramowitz
Mrs. W. H. Alford
F. Monroe Alleman
Martin A. Andersen
Mrs. W. G. Atwood
Mrs. Kenneth Ayala
Mrs. Christina Baldwin
S. C. Battaglia
William Beardall
Stanley Bellows
Mrs. Stanley Bellows
Dr. Clarence Bernstein
William Blanton
Mrs. Joseph Blickman
Nelson R. Boice, Jr.
Mrs. Karl Bolander
Jerome Bornstein
Mrs. Frederick P. Bowden
W. G. Boyd
Ralph Breum
Mrs. George Bullock
Brantley Burcham
Mrs. C. M. Callis
C. Jack Camp
Matilda Campbell
William J. Capehart
Ray Carroll
Mrs. Byron Carter
Mrs. Julian H. Carter
Mrs. Austin A. Caruso
Mrs. Mel Casselberry
Yves Chardon
Mrs. Yves Chardon
F. W. Chase, Jr.
Mrs. Frank Chase
Mrs. George A. Clapham
Mrs. George L. Clapham
LeRoy B. Coffman
Mrs. B. R. Coleman
William Conomos
Mrs. Grady Cooksey
Mrs. S. W. Cooksley
Floyd Cooper
Maj. Gen. M. Fleming Cooper
Mrs. Irving Cox
Robert L. Craig
Robert F. Crane

Mrs. Robert F. Crane
Joseph M. Croson
Joseph Culp
Blair J. Culpepper
Dr. John P. Cummer
Col. Edward G. Davis
Rolland Dean
Dr. Marshall C. Dendy
Mrs. Warner A. Denton
William H. Dial
Mrs. Thomas Dickinson
Thomas B. Drage
Col. Taylor Drysdale
Dr. W. E. Duckwitz
Manly Duckworth
Buell G. Duncan, Jr.
Carl Duncan
Mrs. George F. Dunham
David R. Edgerton
Mrs. Ernest F. Eidlitz
Miss Ann Eidson
Tedford Eidson
Mrs. George L. English
Mrs. John P. Evans
Mrs. Paul Fague
Leonard L. Farber
James H. Fenner
John C. Fosgate
George Foster
John M. Fox
William Frangus
Herman Gade
Lloyd Gahr
Mrs. Homer Gard
Clarence M. Gay
Madame Charlotte Gero
I. B. Gibbs
Will H. Gillett
Mrs. Charles E. Goldberg
Charles E. Goldberg
Dr. James Gollatschek
James L. Goodwin
Mrs. James L. Goodwin
Mrs. Harry Gramm
C. W. Graves, Jr.
Harry Greene
J. G. Grossenbacher

Henri Guertin
Kenneth Guthrie
Paul Guthrie
Charles E. Hagar
Henry Hall
Richard M. Hall
Finley M. Hamilton
Wade L. Hampton
Mrs. I. S. Hankins
Robert M. Harrell
Mrs. E. Burch Hart
Charles J. Hawkins
Walter L. Hays
Mrs. J. L. Hecht
David Hedrick
Robert Heintzelman
John A. Heist
Mrs. Harvey Heller
James Higginbotham
D. A. Highgate
J. D. Holloway
Herbert W. Holm
Dan Honeywell
Mrs. Sara Howden
C. K. Huang
Mrs. Fleming Hubbard
Mrs. Enders P. Huey
Harry C. Hughes
Mrs. Wallace Hughes
Mrs. Dan Hunter
Bessie Dow Huntington
Mrs. William Hupp
John N. Huttig
Joseph Isola
Mrs. Paul P. Jackson
Louis L. Jacobs
Mrs. Bobbie James
Dr. Eugene Jewett
Eugene Kassman
George Camp Keiser
Mrs. George Camp Keiser
William R. Kemp
Carroll Kile
Rodney Kincaid
Joe Scott Kirton
Conway D. Kittredge
Mrs. George Kraft

Richard Lassiter
Mrs. J. E. Laughinghouse
Richard H. Lawrence
Dr. Morton Levy
Charles Limpus
Mrs. Edith Tadd Little
Jerry Lyons
Mrs. Virginia McAllister
William McCord
William A. McCree
Joseph McGovern
Hugh F. McKean
James F. McKey
Edward K. McNeal
J. R. McPherson
Raymer Maguire, Jr.
Stewart Martin
Mrs. Helen H. Mason
Dr. Fred Mathers
Mrs. E. S. Meyer
Mrs. Douglas G. Miller
Coleman Miller
Mrs. Charles Millican
Dr. Helen Moore
Mrs. Stanley F. Morse
Mrs. Leonard Munson
Kyran M. Murphy
Robert B. Murphy
Edmund L. Murray
A. K. Nasrallah, Jr.
Mrs. A. K. Nasrallah, Jr.
Robert Neel
Egbert Neidig
Mrs. George W. Newhart

William G. Newsom, Jr.
Dr. G. H. Opdyke
Dr. Louis Orr
Mrs. Louis Orr
Joseph Padawer
Arthur Pariser
Jeno Paulucci
G. L. Perera
Mrs. Wellborn C. Phillips
Dr. Joseph M. Pipkin
Mrs. Raymond F. Potter
Charles Powers
Mrs. Charles Hyde Pratt
Jack Quello
Miss Charlotte Robinson
Mrs. Arthur F. Rinsky
James H. Robinson
Mrs. Joseph D. Robinson
Mrs. Ford B. Rogers, Jr.
Carl G. Rose
Mrs. W. R. Rosenfelt
Bill D. Saxon
Henry Schenck
Marshall C. Sewall
Myer Shader
Dr. Eugene Shippen
Mrs. Eugene Shippen
W. L. Sims, II
Mrs. W. L. Sims,II
Mrs. Robert H. Skillman
Sidney Smith Jr.
Mrs. Samuel Snelling'
Mrs. A. H. Spivack
C. M. Stanton

Dr. Kenneth R. Steady
Mrs. Joseph Steuer
Hope Strong
Eli Subin
Mrs. George R. Taylor
Mrs. Edward Thaw
Mrs Andrew Townes, Jr
Mrs. Robert Trumbo
Mrs. James Urban
Mrs. Earl J. Vaughan
Dr. Paul Wagner
Robert Wagner
Robert L. Walker
George Ware
Neil Webman
Dr. Donald R. Weeks, Jr.
Harry J. Welch
Mrs. M. Trismen Whitacre
Mrs. Frank Whitmore
C. E. Willard
G. T. Willey
David Wilson
Hamer Wilson
Mrs. Osburn C. Wilson
Morton Wolfe
Norman L. Wolfe
Mrs. Milton P. Woodard
Harvey L. Woodruff
Mrs. Bernhard Yagerman
Mrs. D. Arthur Yergey
D. Arthur Yergey
Robert L. Young
Mrs. William E. Young
Dr. Robert Zellner

1974 — 75

MANAGEMENT

MUSICIANS

and other
SPECIAL PEOPLE

ROBERT L. LANDERS
Executive Vice-President and General Manager

Robert L. Landers, Executive Vice President and General Manager of the Florida Symphony Society, Inc., succeeded to these offices in 1972, after serving for three years as Assistant Manager under Miss Helen E. Ryan. Landers did advanced study in music at Eastman School of Music in Rochester, N. Y., and, in 1939, he began his professional career as Assistant Chorus Master and clarinetist with the San Carlo Opera Company.

Upon being called to military duty in 1941, he was sent to the Army School of Music, and became a Warrant Officer-Bandleader. He led the 529th Air Force Band which, under his leadership, was judged to be the best of the 130 Air Training Command Bands.

Following the war, Mr. Landers became head of the Music Department of the McAllister, Okla., Public Schools, but in 1947 he was asked to rejoin the military to become Director of the now world-famous Singing Sergeants, and Associate Conductor of the U.S. Air Force Band and Symphony Orchestra. One of his duties with the Band and the Singing Sergeants was as tour manager, arranging trips to all states and to fifty-four foreign countries. Thanks to his attention to detail, the groups never missed a curtain-call in eighteen years!

Concurrently with his military duties, Mr. Landers held the post of Head of the Instrumental Music Department of the University of Maryland, and Minister of Music at Eldbrooke Church in Washington, D. C.

Landers retired from active military duty in 1965, and in 1967 moved to Tampa, Florida, for a "restful retirement". In short order, though, he had formed the Tampa Oratorio Society and, with the then existing Tampa Philharmonic, did the Brahms "Requiem", "Elijah", and two "Messiahs". He also prepared the combined Tampa Oratorio Society and a St. Petersburg group for the Beethoven "Ninth Symphony" to climax the first season of the Floida Gulf Coast Symphony.

When the opportunity arose to come to Orlando in 1969 as assistant manager of the Florida Symphony, Landers accepted rapidly. Succeeding to General Managership in 1972, he has even conducted some of the Symphony's Youth concerts and children's concerts, in addition to his other multitudinous duties.

Managing a Symphony Orchestra with a schedule as crowded as that of the Florida Symphony requires an individual with a solid musical background plus a number of managerial and other talents, not the least of which is a great amount of tact. Robert L. Landers has all the qualifications.

The Florida Symphony Orchestra

THESE MUSICIANS COMPRISED THE FLORIDA SYMPHONY ORCHESTRA DURING ITS SILVER ANNIVERSARY SEASON, 1974-75

PAVLE DESPALJ
Music Director/Conductor

FIRST VIOLINS
ALPHONSE CARLO
Concertmaster
MAJA VUKOVIC
Assistant Concertmaster
ROBERT HORAK
Assistant Concertmaster
WALTER CARLSON
HELEN WITTE
MARTHA STRAUB
FREDERIC BALAZS
PATRICIA CORNELL
RICHARD COLLINS
NURHAN ARMAN
TOM MOORE
WILLIAM MALCHIK
RESTEL BELL
AARON BENAR

SECOND VIOLINS
JACOB LEVINE
Principal
LUCY HEIBERG
Assistant Principal
RALPH CARRETTA
VICTOR LIGOTTI
MONYA GILBERT
ALEX RUANO
ISIDORE LEE
NICHOLAS DECOLLIBUS
MATSON TOPPER
MARK PONCH
DOLORES BANOSKY
ARTHUR CONVERSE

VIOLAS
MAX WEISER
Principal
EIJI IKEDA
Assistant Principal
BERNICE LITTLE
GERALDINE GEE
JOSEPH SHERMAN
ANNE BARTLETT
SARKIS DEMIRGIAN
VIRGINIA BENNIE

CELLOS
ARPAD SZOMORU
Principal
CECILE SZOMORU
Assistant Principal

CARL MEYER
NICHOLAS LAMPO
JOSEPH DIMAIO
DAVID HALLMAN
ANNE SCHAFFNER
PATRICIA HOLM

CONTRABASSES
CRAIG JOHNSON
Principal
DANIEL THUNE
Assistant Principal
RUSSELL BROWN
DIANE MCHATTIE
EUGENE HOLM
JOHN VARALLO

FLUTES
LINDA THREATTE
Principal
SAUL CORNELL
SUSAN HARRIS
Assistant Principal

PICCOLO
SUSAN HARRIS

OBOES
JANET MASCARO
Principal
SHERWOOD HAWKINS
DIANE LANG

ENGLISH HORN
DIANE LANG

CLARINETS
PETER HARRIS
Principal
LINNEA NEREIM
Assistant Principal
GORDON O'HARA

E FLAT CLARINET
LINNEA NEREIM

BASS CLARINET
GORDON O'HARA

BASSOONS
JOHN BECK
Principal
TERRY GRUSH
Assistant Principal
CORNELIA BIGGERS

CONTRA BASSOON
CORNELIA BIGGERS

HORNS
ARNOLD MASCARO
Principal
VERLE ORMSBY
CAROLYN MACDOWELL
Assistant Principal
LEIGH HARRIS

TRUMPETS
CHARLES GOTTSCHALK
Principal
WILLIAM ARN
JAMES MILLER
Assistant Principal

TROMBONES
JOSEPH KLINGELHOFFER
Principal
JEFFREY D. KONICEK
BRUCE NELSON
Bass Trombone

TUBA
LEE RICHARDSON

HARP
ROSALIND BECK

PIANO AND CELESTE
KATHERINE CARLO

TIMPANI
LAURA STOTESBERY
Principal

PERCUSSION
ROBERT PETTA
Principal
WILLIAM WANSER
RICHARD SHERRILL

LIBRARIAN
HAROLD LITTLE

PERSONNEL MANAGER
VICTOR LIGOTTI
CHARLES GOTTSCHALK
Assistant

STAGE SUPERVISOR
EUGENE HOLM

190

THE FLORIDA SYMPHONY SOCIETY, INC. WISHES TO EXPRESS ITS GRATITUDE TO THE FOLLOWING INDIVIDUALS AND BUSINESS FIRMS, WHO HELPED MAKE POSSIBLE THE PUBLICATION OF THIS HISTORY . . .

Avie Abramowitz
Mr. & Mrs. John Baker
Mr. & Mrs. Stanley P. Bellows
Combanks Corporation
Mr. & Mrs. Reid Ewing
Dr. & Mrs. Cloyde Fausnaugh
First Federal Savings & Loan Association
   of Orlando
Mr. & Mrs. Paul Hayne, Jr.
Ivey's of Orlando
Mr. & Mrs. George W. Johnson
Mr. & Mrs. Robert B. Kolodney
Mr. & Mrs. Robert L. Landers
McKellar-Braun Cadillac, Inc.
Mr. & Mrs. Edmund L. Murray
Orlando Fashion Square
Orlando Federal Savings and Loan
   Association

Pan American Bank of Orlando
Red Lobster Inns of America, Inc.
Mr. & Mrs. James H. Robinson
Miss Helen Ryan
Mrs. Rosalyn Spencer
Sun First National Bank of Orlando
Mrs. Walter L. Thompson
Mr. John Tiedtke
Walt Disney World
Mr. & Mrs. Harold Ward, III
Washington Shores Federal Savings and
   Loan Association
Winter Park Federal Savings and Loan
   Association
Winter Park Telephone Company

Mrs. Stanley P. Bellows

Carol Bellows is presently a member of the Board of Directors of the Florida Symphony Society, Inc. Funding the publication of this Anniversary History has been, for many months, her 'personal project' — and to this end she has devoted untold hours of time and effort.

Her faith in the attainment of her goal remained steadfast through the darkest of days, and her determination was unshakable. The book now in your hands is lasting proof of this charming lady's ultimate success. The Florida Symphony is deeply indebted to Carol Bellows for having helped so significantly in making the publication of this History not just a dream, but a reality.

AND TO THE FLORIDA SYMPHONY OFFICE STAFF, WHO KEEP THINGS MOVING ALL YEAR ROUND.

MS. JIM BARKER-Administrative Assistant
JEFFREY P. PAISON-Assistant Orchestra Manager
MRS. RUTH KATAUSKAS- Finance and Accounting
MRS. J. EARL FRITZ, JR.-Staff Assistant

INDEX

Page Number

THE SETTING — Where it All Happened 5
FORERUNNERS OF THE FLORIDA SYMPHONY 10
THE FRENCH CONNECTION 19
MUSIC: THE AMERICAN WAY, with Frank Miller 33
THE MAZER YEARS. A Dynamic Period 41
A PERIOD OF TRANSITION 59
THE PRUSSIAN PERIOD — the Herz Years 63
GROWING TOWARD TOMORROW: Pavle Despalj to the Present 73
EIPILOG 88
SYMPHONY PRESIDENTS 93
ARMS OF THE FLORIDA SYMPHONY 117
THE FORD FOUNDATION TRUST 129
ANGELS — BENEFACTORS — SPONSORS 135
APPENDIX 146
MANAGEMENT, MUSICIANS and Other Special People............................. 187